ENDORSEMENTS

I've seen countless entrepreneurs leave money on the table due to fear and uncertainty in pricing. *Fearless Pricing* is more than just a roadmap to higher profits; it's a manifesto for being justly paid for the full value you deliver.

—Gino Wickman
Author of *Traction* & *Shine*
Creator of EOS® (Entrepreneurial Operating System®)

This book is a wake-up call. If you're delivering excellence, stop accepting mediocre pay. Price your services to truly reflect your value and unlock the rewards you deserve. A must-read for anyone ready to claim their worth.

—Mel Robbins
Bestselling Author and Host, The Mel Robbins Podcast

In the game of pricing poker, Casey Brown is the ultimate shark. Her book is THE must-have pricing playbook, providing business leaders with practical, proven strategies to level up organizational confidence and create real value for buyers and sellers.

—Jennifer Zick
Founder & CEO, Authentic®

Fearless Pricing demystifies the art of pricing with practical ideas, relatable examples, and real-life stories, making it accessible and actionable. This book will not only transform your pricing strategy but also deliver a massive return on your investment in time and money, with the potential to generate thousands in additional revenue by implementing just one idea.

—Rob Dube
Visionary, The 10 Disciplines

I can't believe how much money we have made from Casey Brown's ideas about pricing! If you've ever had a customer say that your price was too high, you need to read *Fearless Pricing*.

—Ray Crook
President, Quantum Services

There is not a more profitable way to spend a few hours this week than absorbing and applying the pricing genius of Casey Brown, self-avowed pricing geek. From the CEO to the sales professional, Casey's insights, strategies, and tactics are a masterclass in turning the fears of pricing into a powerful statement of your value to your customer.

—Joe Galvin
Chief Research Officer, Vistage International

Casey's insights in *Fearless Pricing* have had a marked impact in our company to the tune of millions of dollars, but more importantly to the feeling of accomplishment for hundreds of employees. For decades, Casey discovered and pioneered methods to make pricing your strategic advantage, and now she has distilled that wisdom and expertise into *Fearless Pricing*. Read it. It will change your life.

—Bob Domnick
CEO, Superior Industries & Lincoln Office

Fearless Pricing is a powerful companion to the core principles of EOS®. At the heart of every successful business lies the ability to stay true to its vision, remain disciplined in its execution, and hold core values close. Casey's insights into pricing and negotiation align beautifully with these principles, laying out a path for leaders to make informed, confident choices about the value they provide in alignment with core values. Her approach empowers companies to stay focused on their most important work while being compensated fairly for excellence.

—Mark O'Donnell
Visionary, EOS® Worldwide

Casey Brown turns pricing from a challenge into a powerful opportunity. *Fearless Pricing* is packed with invaluable strategies that deliver real impact. Highly recommended!

—Sue Hawkes
Expert EOS Implementer™ and CEO, YESS!

Casey offers a fresh perspective on pricing that every B2B leader needs to hear. *Fearless Pricing* shows how to make pricing your competitive advantage.

—Andrew Ellerhorst
President & CEO, JDXpert

If there's a person who knows pricing better than Casey Brown, I don't know of them. She has made pricing her life's work, and this engaging book is one more step in her journey in proving pricing's undervalued role in business. Come along for the ride; you won't regret it.

—Timmy McCarthy
Former Franchisee, Raising Cane's

Fearless Pricing has quickly become our go-to guide on pricing strategy. This isn't another boring textbook that requires a degree in economics to understand. Casey's use of story makes pricing principles easy to understand and even keeps a creative, ADHD-minded business owner engaged. In just a short time after implementing the *Fearless Pricing* approach, our profitability increased by over 30%.

—Beth Menduni
Founder & Chief Storyteller, Video Story Studio

If you want to change your life, change your price. Tips and tricks are an understatement when it comes to the page-turning power delivered in *Fearless Pricing*. This is a must-read for every entrepreneur, a step-by-step resource that will change your life and business forever.

—Dave Wescott
CEO, Evergreen Brands

Fearless Pricing is a practical guide to unlocking pricing power. Our company now has a culture and common language around pricing strategy that provides us with a profitable, sustainable business in a competitive environment.

—Michael Berman
President, US Event Rentals, Arena Group

Casey's content has completely reshaped our franchisees' viewpoint on our pricing power rooted in our value. Strategies outlined in *Fearless Pricing* for overcoming discount pressures and negotiating with confidence are invaluable. This book offers a fresh perspective on pricing that every business leader should embrace to drive profitability and sustainable growth.

—Tom Wood
President & CEO, Floor Coverings International

The insights in *Fearless Pricing* are both revolutionary and practical, providing actionable steps that have the power to transform pricing and negotiations. If you want to help your team maximize profits through better pricing, this book is a must-read.

—Catherine Lang-Cline
CEO, Portfolio Creative

This book taught my team to see pricing as a strategic advantage, not a necessary evil. Casey Brown brings clarity to one of the most challenging aspects of business.

—Bryan Cousino
Principal, Salas O'Brien

Casey Brown's expertise in pricing has been a game-changer for many, including one of my own clients, who, thanks to her guidance, added over $500k to their bottom line. Her unique ability to blend art, science, and psychology into pricing strategies sets her apart, making her one of the most brilliant minds in the industry today. Read *Fearless Pricing*.

—Ryan Tansom
Speaker & Coach, Independence by Design

Casey's insights are practical, actionable, and proven to help you win in pricing. It is not often a business book comes along that can have an IMMEDIATE impact on your top and bottom line and your ability to better serve your customers. This is it! *Fearless Pricing* is a brilliant resource for anyone looking to elevate their pricing game AND meaningfully improve their business.

—Kurt Theriault
President, Allied Executives

Casey's vision, like her book, is spot on. The mindset of the seller is everything when it comes to margin. She challenged our team, and they increased gross margins 2 percent in the first year on $100 million in B2B with 10 percent growth in volume. Now, we run well above our industry average GP percent. Worth the read for your whole team.

—Bill Lucken
Eastern Vice President of Sales,
Associated Packaging, Inc.

The tactics in *Fearless Pricing* helped us increase our margins significantly. If you want to enhance your skills, shift your mindset, and boost profitability, read this book!
—Elizabeth Blount McCormick
CEO, Uniglobe Travel Designers

Fearless Pricing offers a clear, compelling approach to mastering pricing in today's market. Casey Brown makes the topic approachable, understandable, and—dare I say—exciting. This book will guide you into a pricing strategy that guarantees you're compensated for the value you bring. Read it and get into the groove of setting prices with confidence!
—Victoria Cabot
Head of Community, EOS® Worldwide

Fearless Pricing is more than just a guide—it's a powerful movement that empowers everyone, especially those from marginalized and underrepresented groups, to confidently command the prices that reflect their true worth. Casey's book empowers people to confidently take ownership of their worth—such a crucial shift for those who have historically been underpaid or undervalued. It serves as a much-needed coach, ensuring that you are seen, heard, and valued at every step.
—Lachandra Baker
Founder & Workforce Optimization Strategist,
Lachandra B. Baker Edutainment, LLC

Fearless Pricing is a treasure trove of wisdom for CEOs. Casey's approach is both refreshing and imminently practical.
—Michael Black
President, Struers

Fearless Pricing will make you rethink everything you know about pricing and value. Casey's wisdom on pricing is unmatched.

—Kristie Clayton
Founder & CEO, HERverse

Working with CEOs, it long ago became obvious that prices, and the inherent fear of raising them, was of critical concern. Enter Casey Brown. Her book, *Fearless Pricing*, amplifies and expands her in-person presentations that cleared concerns of imagined consequences, resulting in increased flow of black ink to the bottom line. Over the course of more than 30 years chairing CEO groups, I've heard and read the best thinking of literally hundreds of speakers and authors; I rate Casey among the very best in both categories.

—Bud Carter
Senior Chair, Vistage International

Casey teaches you to stop competing on price and start selling on value. This book is going to help a lot of companies.

—Eric Rozenberg
President & CEO, Event Business Formula

I have shifted my mindset as a result of the ideas in *Fearless Pricing*. Our conversations with customers are more focused on value and impact, and our sales conversations feel more like partnerships now.

—Christy Clement
Co-Founder, fluent

Casey's strategies have given us the confidence to ask for the prices we deserve and not look back. Our leadership

team now prioritizes pricing as an instrumental piece of our profit strategy, and pricing is part of our culture. If you want to increase your profit margins, start with *Fearless Pricing*.
—Bill Zaruka
President & CEO, Wedgewood Weddings & Events

Fearless Pricing will help every business leader looking to get serious about their pricing performance. In a world where too many companies race to the bottom, Casey reminds us all that 'good' is not good enough and that pricing excellence starts with confidence and courage in your value. She offers a playbook filled with practical tools, real-world examples, and a whole lot of tough love—because it's time to stop letting customers dictate your worth. Casey's approach is a wake-up call, challenging every reader to rethink their pricing mindset and transform their results. It's time to stop selling yourself short, and this book shows you exactly how to do it.
—Rik Vonderhaar
Transition Specialist for Privately-Held and Family-Owned Businesses

Casey Brown's work cuts through any head trash and limiting beliefs around the value of our work. *Fearless Pricing* offers a transformative approach to assigning value to your work, grounded in her highly-rated TED Talk that has been viewed millions of times. She is the voice in my ear saying, "You are worth more than that!" Over the years, her teachings have empowered me to charge what we're truly worth. By simply pulling this pricing lever, we have been able to exponentially grow our business, leading to both record profitability and client satisfaction.
—Sarah Irvin Clark
President & Owner, Irvin Public Relations

Fearless Pricing is a game-changer for anyone looking to transform their pricing strategy. The insights are not only practical but empowering, helping you move past hesitation and set prices with confidence. Casey has provided our members a new and much needed perspective on pricing which helps CEOs and their teams to stop leaving money on the table.

—Carol Butler
President, Goering Center for
Family & Private Business

Nothing impacts your bottom line more than raising price! Casey's approach gives you confidence and motivation to demand what you are worth. Priceless!

—Jeff Dudan
CEO, Homefront Brands

I feel so fortunate to have met Casey Brown at a time when my company was struggling to protect margins. The investment to have Casey present at Caster Concepts was recaptured in the first month. A small price to pay for a value that continues to pay back today. Caster Concepts has never looked back. Casey's message in *Fearless Pricing* is powerful, applicable, and spot-on when it comes to selling. Thanks, Casey, for sharing your passion for appropriate pricing of our products.

—Bill Dobbins
Owner, Caster Concepts Inc.

Casey Brown breaks down pricing myths and replaces them with profitable truths. This book is a wake-up call for any business underpricing their value.

—Alec Broadfoot
CEO, VisionSpark

This book is a masterclass in pricing execution. We've used Casey's clear, actionable insights to help our sales team overcome common pricing challenges and negotiate with newfound confidence. Her guidance and deep expertise proved to be applicable to everything from the smallest of challenges to the largest of complex, global pricing situations. Casey gives a memorable new meaning to the phrase 'hot sauce.'

—Chris Manning
President, The Shepherd Color Company

Casey's book has been a revelation for our pricing execution. Her strategies are not just powerful—they're transformative.

—Gray Sherrill
M.G. Newell Corporation

Finally, a step-by-step guide for every entrepreneurial sales team to gain confidence in pricing by returning to their true value. Follow this book and watch profits grow!

—Matt Hahne
Certified EOS Implementer™ & Founder,
The Supervisor Playbook

Casey Brown is fired up about pricing! As a passionate advocate for entrepreneurs and their teams to get paid for their excellence, she shares advice that is direct, practical, actionable, and makes a huge difference. Reading this book is like having Casey as your personal pricing coach.

—Alex Freytag
Expert EOS Implementer™ & Creator, ProfitWorks

FEARLESS PRICING

Ignite Your Team, Own Your Value,
and Command What You Deserve

TABLE OF CONTENTS

FOREWORD
BY GINO WICKMAN

Mastering pricing is akin to unlocking a secret code, revealing hidden opportunities for profit and growth that most businesses overlook. Casey Brown's *Fearless Pricing* lays out the blueprint to harness its full potential.

In the ever-evolving landscape of business, one constant remains: the need to capture the true value of your products and services. In my decades of work with entrepreneurs, I've seen countless businesses struggle with pricing, often leaving money on the table due to fear, uncertainty, and inability to defend value. Casey's book is the answer.

Casey and I have shared the stage on several occasions, and I can attest to the power and clarity of her message. Her insights into pricing are not only practical but transformative. Casey brings a unique blend of engineering precision, deep psychological understanding, and a passion for helping businesses thrive. *Fearless Pricing* showcases her expertise and her unwavering commitment to helping organizations unlock their true potential.

This book masterfully blends mindset and skillset, equipping you with the confidence and the technical acumen necessary to excel. This combination provides a powerful toolkit for achieving pricing excellence.

> MINDSET: This book reveals the mindset barriers to confident pricing, addressing deep-seated fears and offering tools to overcome them. By tackling self-limiting beliefs at the root of most pricing decision-making, Casey equips you to stand firm on your value and negotiate with courage. Her approach transforms fear into confidence, ensuring that you can command the prices your excellence deserves.

> SKILL SET: *Fearless Pricing* is a practical guide for effective pricing execution. Casey illuminates common customer tactics and practical countermeasures to combat those tactics. She lays out a path to conquer discounts, which are often fueled by unwarranted fear of losing sales volume. She equips you with cutting-edge tools and value-based frameworks to identify pricing opportunities, make better pricing decisions, and make more money.

Throughout this book, you'll find a blend of strategic insights, practical advice, and motivational guidance. It's not just a roadmap to improve profits; it's about ensuring you are justly paid for the profound value you deliver to your customers. Casey's passion for the subject shines through every page, making complex concepts accessible and actionable.

As you read these pages, I encourage you to embrace Casey's teachings with an open mind and a willingness to challenge your existing beliefs about pricing. The principles have the power to transform your business, elevating your pricing confidence and driving substantial profit growth. This book is an essential read for any business leader serious about capturing the true value of their offerings. Her insights provide a strategic blueprint for pricing success. I have no doubt that *Fearless Pricing* will be a catalyst for growth and profitability in your business.

Prepare to be challenged, inspired, and equipped to price confidently and command the prices you deserve. With Casey's expert guidance, you'll transform fear into confidence, challenges into opportunities, and ordinary profits into extraordinary growth. Dive into this book, absorb its wisdom, and watch your business transform.

—Gino Wickman
Author of *Traction* and *Shine*
Creator of EOS® (Entrepreneurial Operating System®)

INTRODUCTION

I love pricing. I *love* pricing. Nothing in school, by the way, prepared me for how cool pricing is. I took an econ class, and I learned about the demand curve:

The demand curve tells us if you charge more, you sell less; if you charge less, you sell more. Simple math. This is a very straightforward explanation of how pricing works.

But that's not how it is in the real world. Once I saw how pricing really worked and negotiations really unfold, I understood that pricing is far less straightforward. It's more nuanced, unpredictable, and mysterious. It's the intersection of art and science.

Pricing is like poker: everybody's bluffing. Sellers try to hide how little they're willing to accept. Buyers hide how much they're willing to pay. Everybody assesses the strength of their own hand and guesses at the strength of their opponent's.

And who wins the poker game in the buyer-seller relationship? Typically, the buyer. Why? Because both sides buy into the illusion that the buyer has the stronger hand.

But often, the buyer is bluffing. Not only that, but the seller has a strong hand to play. Do you believe in what you sell? Do you solve real problems for your customers? Do you deliver excellence and valuable products and services to your customers? If you do, then you have a strong hand to play.

Your customers are going to buy these products and services from someone. *Why not from you?*

Why Pricing?

In the following chapters, I'll share why I believe businesses should focus more time and attention on pricing. But why is this the focus of my whole career?

For me, pricing is mission-driven work. If you're excellent at what you do—if you deliver excellent products and services to your customers—then you ought to be paid like you're excellent. Not like you're good, and certainly not like you're mediocre. And I find that companies are chronically underpricing, at least in some areas of their business.

Many of your products and services to many of your customers on many of your opportunities may be priced exactly right. But if *any* of your prices on *any* of your products and services on *any* of your opportunities to *any* of your customers are less than they could be, then you're accepting mediocre pay for excellent work.

This fires me up. I cannot abide this because I know what it takes to deliver excellence. It takes hard work, passion, dedication, commitment, years of building expertise, risk-taking, long hours, creativity, reinvestment, and deep relationships with your customers.

> You're accepting mediocre pay for excellent work.

Your competition does not compete with you on quality, service, or excellence. You do not need to compete with them on price. And this is what gives me the fire in my belly to travel around the world talking with business leaders about pricing. Because to accept mediocre pay for excellent work is unjust. *Underpricing is unjust.* Not just for you but also for every person who works in your organization.

It's unjust because it's robbing your organization of the resources that you earn every day with your hard work and your passion and your quality, resources that you could deploy to grow, to innovate, to add new lines of business, to open new facilities, to buy more equipment, to hire more people, to make an acquisition, or to invest in inventory, technology, or better service. What would be possible inside your organization if you didn't accept mediocre pay for excellent work? You could also pay yourself and your people better. What would be possible for the families and communities who depend on those paychecks? This is what's at stake.

This is my *why*. It's about dollars and cents, absolutely. But more importantly, it's about interacting with entrepreneurs, business leaders, and salespeople who pour their hearts out every day for an exquisite customer experience and exceptional quality and seeing that go unrewarded. This is why I'll never stop talking about pricing.

> Accepting mediocre pay for excellent work is unjust, and it's robbing you of resources to grow.

It's pathological for me. Everywhere I go, I leave higher prices in my wake. Here's an example: I went to a new salon for a haircut. The owner of the salon and I made small talk while I was waiting for my stylist. She asked, "So, what do you do?"

"Oh, I'm a pricing consultant."

"Never heard of it. What's that all about?"

"I help people get paid well for excellence."

"Cool. Tell me more!"

The next time I got a haircut there, it was $5 more! (I have to start telling people I'm an accountant or something. Telling the truth is costing me too much money.)

Why I Wrote This Book

I founded Boost Pricing, a pricing training and consulting firm, to help sales teams negotiate from confidence, handle price objections masterfully, and be fearless about price increases.

Over the past 25 years, first in corporate America and then running Boost, I've learned that most pricing decisions are made from fear, not from confidence. Instead of pricing to win, most sellers price not to lose. Even with a perfect pricing strategy, margins still shrink in the face of out-of-control discounting and fear-based pricing.

Does any of this sound familiar?

- Sellers discount too frequently, deeply, broadly, and quickly.
- Salespeople negotiate harder with their manager than with the customers.
- Price increases send your sales team into a panic.
- Sellers cave in too easily to price objections.
- Salespeople discount when compared to inferior competition.
- Fear of losing the deal causes your sales team to "prediscount" quotes before presenting them to the customer.

If pricing and margin worries keep you up at night, you aren't alone.

Between helping hundreds of companies' sales teams maximize profitable sales and delivering keynote talks to over 25,000 business owners, I've learned that owner frustration and lack of sales team confidence about pricing are nearly universal.

Because profit is the lifeblood of business and pricing is a big profit lever, most business leaders will tell me they already pay attention to and care about pricing. However, many feel a sense of anxiety or even helplessness about pricing; whether because of stiff competition, commoditized industries, or sales teams that can't or won't hold the line, they don't see a path to improvement. After hearing my talk or engaging Boost for training, they see how much unrealized pricing opportunity they have to unlock enormous profit lift and (more importantly) how to take advantage of the opportunity.

I wrote this book because I no longer want to spread the message solely to one audience or one client at a time. Remember, this is mission-driven work for me. I want to get the word out: you can get higher prices for your products and services! You can, and you should. You deserve to be paid well for your excellence.

About This Book

In this book, I seek to demystify the true causes of underpricing, pull back the curtain on customer negotiation tactics designed to trigger discounts, and launch you onto a path to improve pricing and dramatically increase profits.

This book is for business owners and leaders who oversee sales teams with pricing discretion and discount authority. As one of those leaders, you understand and believe in the value of your products and services. You believe your team is leaving money on the table through unnecessary discounting and fear-based pricing, and you're looking for ways to achieve the profitability you deserve.

I've organized this book into five parts:

WHY IT MATTERS

PART 1: WHY PRICING?
1. The Power of Pricing
2. Discounts Kill Profits
3. Price-Volume Relationship

WHAT THEY DO

PART 2: CUSTOMER TACTICS
4. Tactic or Market Intel?
5. What Does "Yes" Mean?
6. "Your Price is Too High"

PART 3: PRICING OPPORTUNITIES
7. Customer Buying Criteria
8. Identifying the Hot Sauce

PART 4: PRICING FOR VALUE

9. Why They Buy
10. Solve a Problem
11. Don't Signal Low Quality
12. Price Objection How-To
13. Cost of Failure
14. Give to Get

WHAT YOU CAN DO

PART 5: EXECUTING ON STRATEGY
15. Tools to Identify Opportunity
16. Tools for Smart Decisions

Part 1, "Why Pricing?," begins with the most fundamental aspect of the power of pricing: the pulley effect, or how small increases have a huge profit lift. (If you're already versed in the concept of "The Power of 1 Percent," please *do not* skip this section. This section is not about the math but, instead, offers a very different take on this oft-discussed topic.) We dive into the flipside of that coin—how small discounts kill profits—and into common traps for salespeople in price negotiations, how sellers give in to discounting when they shouldn't, and how to approach discounting when price concessions truly are necessary. We wrap up Part 1 with a look at the price-volume relationship—a frequently misunderstood concept that leads to unnecessary discounting and fear-driven decisions in pricing and selling.

In Part 2, "Customer Tactics," we look at common customer tactics to get your products and services for less. Some mistakes sellers make when confronting these tactics include confusing buying strategies with market intel, only paying attention to when they hear *no* from customers, and folding under the pressure of "Your price is too high."

How to counter customer tactics is the focus of the next two parts:

- Part 3: "Pricing Opportunities"
- Part 4: "Pricing for Value"

Part 3 explores the unexpected pricing opportunities presented by uncovering and leveraging differing price sensitivities of your customers and of your products and services. Where is price sensitivity low, and how can you tap into that?

In Part 4, we demonstrate that the best countermeasure to price sensitivity is pricing for value and ensuring that the messaging you wrap around your sales process helps you extract the highest price for the value you deliver. In this part, we illustrate how to lower price sensitivity through relentless focus on customer value.

Finally, in Part 5, we look at how to ensure that pricing execution matches your pricing strategy. Spending time, effort, and money on pricing strategy is completely wasted in the hands of a sales force that doesn't get it, agree with it, or execute it. One way to ensure that your salespeople are executing your pricing strategy is by implementing and using data tools. In this final section, I present seven tools and how they can help your team uncover opportunities in pricing.

Throughout the book, you'll read stories from Boost Pricing clients and audience members who have implemented what they learned in our training and keynote talks and can speak firsthand about how it has impacted their profitability. You'll also find QR codes throughout the book to download powerful, free tools, worksheets, and templates to use with your sales team to practice these ideas and apply them to your own business.

If you wish to save some time and steps, you can download all the free resources in one zip file:

A Word to Salespeople

Because I know some business leaders will ply their sales teams with this book, I want to offer a few comments to salespeople reading it.

In my experience, the biggest obstacles to pricing success aren't competition, customers, insufficient business knowledge, lack of strategy, or lack of sophisticated cost and pricing analysis. It's self-limiting beliefs and behaviors that sabotage pricing success. This book will crack open those beliefs and behaviors and then arm you with methods, messaging, tools, and confidence to communicate, defend, and negotiate higher prices for the value of the products and services you provide.

Sales is hard—one of the hardest jobs in any company. Generally, when things go right with the customer, they aren't pouring praise all over you, allowing you to bask in the glory of exquisite service. But when things go wrong, you get all the blame. Not only that, but you have to go out into the world and take the proverbial customer beatings over price during negotiations. You have to be the bearer of bad news at price increase time. On top of all of that, too many of your coworkers dismiss the value of your role and even your profession. They might even make jokes about how you spend your time golfing and relaxing over lunch with customers. You put up with a lot to be in sales!

If, at any point reading this book, you feel like I'm taking a shot at salespeople, I want you to remember this: I have incredible respect for the hard work and value that salespeople bring. Without sales, no one in the company has a job or gets a paycheck. The work you do matters. It's valuable. It's honorable. And my guess is, simply based on the fact that you are reading this book, you are already an open-minded, successful seller who wants to be the best you can be.

Almost every salesperson we train at Boost is the same: they are already experts in their industry, company, products, services, and customers. They already know how to sell and price and do so successfully each day. The same is true for any reader of this book. The goal is simply to add to your existing sales skill set and mindset so you can be even *more* successful and make even *more* money. If that's a goal you can align with, I believe you'll find a lot of value in these pages.

An Invitation to Confidence in Pricing

Jack Welch said, "Costs are a matter of fact; pricing is a matter of guts." I think it's true, but I say it a little bit differently. I say pricing is a matter of confidence.

You don't need to go to your customers, hat in hand, terrified or apologetic about charging a fair price for the products and services you sell. You can have the confidence that, despite the tactics your customers use, they *do* value the products and services you sell. You can have the confidence that, despite those tactics, they are willing to pay you a fair price for them—and anything else is unjust.

Pricing is a matter of confidence.

Not so sure? Read on.

PART 1

WHY PRICING?

Most businesses are incredibly focused on sales growth. They have sales leaders, sales teams, sales metrics and reports, sales meetings, sales initiatives, sales contests, and so on. It's the same on the operational side of their business—they are trying to manage costs, cut down on waste, and procure smarter.

In my keynote talks, I ask audience members to raise their hands if they are having regular sales meetings. Nearly every hand goes up. I ask about operations and cost-management meetings. Same.

Then, I ask: "How many of you are having regular strategic pricing meetings?" A smattering of hands. Some nervous laughter from the majority of the room, with their hands in their laps.

I don't do this to blame or shame anyone but to help them see the opportunity in front of them because pricing is the biggest financial lever we have. There is no greater impact on profitability for any organization than a price change. But in my experience, companies are laser-focused on growing sales volume and managing costs and far less focused on being more strategic with pricing.

Pricing gets the least focus and attention in nearly every business I encounter. I suggest that businesses start a cadence of strategic price meetings. Under the adage of "what gets measured gets done," the very act of shining a light on pricing practices, structure, processes, and metrics will change behavior, which will change results.

Pricing gets the least focus and attention in nearly every business.

We are killing ourselves to grow sales volume with existing customers. And we have both feet on the gas pedal, bleeding and sweating in the marketplace to win new customers. I am, by no means, saying that we should take our foot off the gas pedal; rather, give just a bit more attention to pricing.

Give pricing a seat at the table. I know sales is king; sales will always have the throne. But pull up a stool for pricing. There isn't anything you can do in your business that will make a bigger impact on your profits than increasing pricing focus and mastery.

In Part 1, we're going to look at why pricing is the biggest financial lever you have in your business. To do that, we'll focus on three truths:

1. Small price increases will give you a huge profit lift.
2. Small discounts will kill your profits.
3. Sales volume loss from a price change is overestimated.

We'll examine each of these ideas in the next three chapters. I'll share stories from my own clients, audiences, and the wider business world along with real-world data to show how these truths play out in companies. This will set the stage for Part 2, where we look at what customers do in price negotiations to get what you sell for less.

CHAPTER 1

THE POWER OF PRICING

Learning Objectives

1. Understand the profound impact of small pricing increases on overall profitability.
2. Recognize the common disconnect between theoretical pricing knowledge and practical application necessary to capture the full potential of pricing power.
3. Discover the concept of pricing as a "pulley" to effortlessly lift profits with minimal increases.

Before we get started, I want to set one thing straight. I know that, as a business leader, you understand the power of small price increases. I know you know, fundamentally, the power of 1 percent. That's not why I believe so strongly that you need this book and that it can help you.

One of the most challenging aspects of the work our company does is helping business leaders see what they already know *in a different light*—how to apply the pricing knowledge they already have for real profit gains. They *know* what pricing techniques have worked in the past. They *know* the pain of losing deals over price. They *know* the competitive landscape and its impact on pricing. They've been doing this for so long they don't need us to teach them about the power of 1 percent. The problem is *they're not doing it.*

There is a disconnect between what companies think they're doing and what they're actually doing, resulting in a failure to fully leverage their pricing power to capture the opportunities in front of them. Clients and keynote audiences eye me with skepticism when I tell them that they are leaving money on the table and how much it's costing them. I can actually *feel* their effort not to roll their eyes. (As the mother of teenage daughters, I've become very adept at reading these not-so-subtle cues.)

There is no greater impact on profitability for any organization than pricing.

So, I invite you to stifle your inner groan when I tell you something you already know:

> There is no greater impact on profitability
> for any organization than pricing.

A 1 percent increase in pricing has a bigger impact on your profitability than a 1 percent increase in sales volume or a 1 percent reduction in expenses.

I call pricing the pulley for your business. A pulley is a simple machine that works on the basis of mechanical advantage: apply a small amount of force to lift a large amount of weight. In the simplest terms, a pulley makes it easier to lift something.

Pricing works the same way. It is the simple financial machine that makes it easier for companies to lift profits. Apply a small price increase to generate a large profit lift.

When I talk to business leaders about this concept, they tell me that they understand it, but their team has already been trained on it. Sometimes, several times. We know they're thinking, *Oh no, they're not going to teach me the power of 1 percent again, are they?* And the answer, every time, is yes, we are. Because it's not just about understanding the concept on an intellectual level and teaching it to your sales teams. It's knowing it *and* feeling the gut punch of leaked profits in a personal, visceral way. It's keeping it top of mind and applying it in the day-to-day process of pricing and selling.

> **Sales teams know the power of 1 percent, but they aren't applying it consistently, rigorously, conscientiously every day, with every customer, every time.**

We see, in our work with businesses, that this concept often gets lost in the shuffle of everyday operations—sales teams *think* they are applying it, but they are running on autopilot, falling back on old habits and rules of thumb that work against their success. They get the concept, they know the power of 1 percent, but they aren't applying it consistently, rigorously, conscientiously every day, with every customer, every time.

Let's look at an illustration of the pricing pulley that applies to every business, no matter what you sell or who your customers are.

The World's Simplest P&L

Take a company with a 5 percent bottom line. For every dollar that customers give this company for their products or services, 95 cents go back to pay the employees, the cost of the facility, raw materials, insurance, electricity, trucks—whatever it takes for them to serve their customers. At the end of the day, the company keeps five cents.

Consider a Company with 5% Net Profit:

REVENUE $1.00

- COST $0.95

PROFIT $0.05

Now, let's say this company increases the price by just 1 percent. (Of the thousands of people I've surveyed about increasing prices by 1 percent, over 90 percent said they would lose less than 5 percent of sales volume.)

How much more costly is it to serve their customers with a price increase? Zero. It doesn't cost any more for them on rent, utilities, raw materials, labor, insurance, or anything else. So, revenue increases to $1.01; the five cents turns into six cents. Because revenue increased without incremental cost, the entire $0.01 dropped to the bottom line. One cent on top of five cents represents a *20 percent increase* in their profitability.

It's so simple that it bears repeating: A 1 percent change in price results in a 20 percent lift on profit. This is the pulley effect of pricing.

Every percentage point of price is a mountain of gold on the bottom line.

1% Price Change Drives 20% Profit Change 20% Profit Change

+ REVENUE $1.01

- COST $0.95

+ PROFIT $0.06

If this same company can increase prices by 5 percent, revenue increases to $1.05. With no change to expenses, the $0.05 drops to the bottom line, *doubling* it. A 100 percent change in profit from just a 5 percent change in price is more than just exciting—it's transformative.

5% Price Change Drives 100% Profit Change

 + **REVENUE $1.05**

 **- COST $0.95**

 + **PROFIT $0.10**

Perhaps you don't have a 5 percent bottom line. Yours could be 2 percent or 10 percent or 50 percent. Regardless of how big or small your profit is today, the principle still applies. By raising your price even a small amount, you increase your profitability significantly.

It's a no-brainer, right? But even this simple example can result in a lot of pushback. We often hear one (or more) of these four objections to raising prices:

1. "It's just 1 or 2 percent—is it even worth it?"
2. "I can't do big price increases."
3. "It's easier to grow profits by selling more."
4. "We know this math already!"

I want to look at each of these objections in turn, so I can show you how to think differently about them.

"It's Just 1 or 2 Percent — Is It Even Worth It?"

A common refrain from business leaders, sales leaders, and those on the front lines of selling and pricing is "It's just 1 or 2 percent"—in other words, it's so small that it's not even worth doing. We hear "It's just $100 on a $10,000 order." Or "It's just $0.01 on a $1/pound product." Or "It's just $1 on a $100/hour service." These sound like rounding errors, but you can see from the chart below that 1 or 2 percent makes a massive difference on the bottom line.

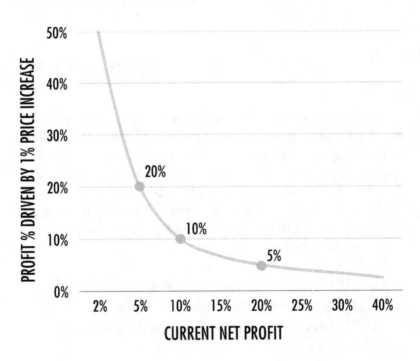

Figure 1.1 Percentage profit lift from 1 percent price increase based on bottom-line profit

So, if you have a 10 percent bottom-line profit:

- 1% price increase = 10% bottom-line profit increase
- 2% price increase = 20% bottom-line profit increase
- 5% price increase = 50% bottom-line profit increase
- 10% price increase = 100% bottom-line profit increase

What does this look like for your business? Table 1.1 illustrates what a 1 percent price increase would translate to in bottom-line profit for your business, depending on your starting point of profitability.

NET PROFIT	PROFIT LIFT FROM 1% PRICE
1%	100%
2%	50%
3%	33%
4%	25%
5%	20%
6%	17%
7%	14%
8%	13%
9%	11%
10%	10%
11%	9%
12-13%	8%
14-15%	7%
16-18%	6%
19-22%	5%
23-28%	4%
29-40%	3%
41-66%	2%
67% +	1%

Table 1.1 Impact to bottom-line profit
from a 1 percent price increase

The simple formula is:

$$\% \, Change \, to \, Bottom - Line \, Profit = \frac{Price \, Increase \, \%}{Initial \, Bottom - Line \, Profit}$$

Power of Price Exercise

Make sure you and your team know the powerful impact of a small change in price by calculating the Power of Price.

1. Start by filling in blank A at the top, the bottom-line profitability of your organization. ("Bottom-line profit" could be net operating income, EBITDA, or whatever you use to measure net profitability for your business. The pricing lesson and the calculations are the same.)

2. Locate the number you just wrote down in blank A on the left side of Table 1.1 to get the corresponding profit lift on the right side. Write your profit lift number into blank B. For every percentage point of price you gain, your net profit improves by this number.

3. Next, fill in Table C at the bottom, which summarizes the impact of 1, 2, 5, and 10 percent price increases for your business.

A. NET PROFIT % (OR EBITDA, OPERATING PROFIT, ETC.)

_____%

B. FOR EVERY PERCENT OF PRICE, PROFIT IMPROVES BY:

_____%

C.

NET PROFIT	PROFIT LIFT FROM 1% PRICE
1%	
2%	
5%	
10%	

Here's an example of the exercise completed by one of our clients with a 13 percent bottom-line profit:

A. NET PROFIT % (OR EBITDA, OPERATING PROFIT, ETC.)

_____*13*_____%

B. FOR EVERY PERCENT OF PRICE, PROFIT IMPROVES BY:

_____*8*_____%

C.

NET PROFIT	PROFIT LIFT FROM 1% PRICE
1%	*8%*
2%	*16%*
5%	*40%*
10%	*80%*

Download a fillable PDF of the Power of Price Worksheet here:

For most businesses, a 1 percent price lift results in a double-digit increase in profit. It's a big deal.

Regardless of your current profitability, it's critical that you and your sales team know this number. Arming your sales team with knowledge, understanding, and skill to apply this powerful insight will improve your financial performance dramatically.[†]

> **For most businesses, a 1 percent price lift results in a double-digit increase in profit.**

[†]   *Note:* If you're worried about sharing detailed financials with your sales team, there's a workaround. Instead of giving them the nitty-gritty numbers, why not use hypotheticals or industry standards to show how pricing impacts profits? This way, you're keeping your specific financials under wraps while still getting the crucial point across: pricing decisions really matter.

That said, I implore you to consider sharing this information. In the absence of information, your people invent information. My experience with hundreds of sales teams in the dark? They often believe that you are much more profitable than you actually are. Sharing profitability in the format shown in this chapter means hitting the highlights of the profit picture, not distributing your P&L to everyone on the team! Letting your sales team in on the company's overall profit performance is a win-win. They can align

How much profit is gained or lost with a 1 percent change in price? It should be your foremost concern when you're making selling and pricing decisions.

If this number is top-of-mind, your salespeople can do quick mental math when faced with pricing opportunities to calculate the dramatic impact. Otherwise, it's too easy to dismiss "small" price changes as insignificant, when, in fact, they are just the opposite.

"I Can't Do Big Price Increases"

Another argument against increasing prices is "I can't do big price increases. You don't understand how competitive and commoditized my industry is." The fear is that a price change of 5 or 10 percent will cost the company sales volume.

But pricing is a game of fractions. A price increase doesn't have to be large to make an impact on your bottom line. It doesn't have to be 10 or even 5 percent. It can be 2 percent, or 1 percent, or 0.5 percent. Half a percent will still result in double-digit bottom-line growth for businesses with a 20 percent bottom-line profit.

Here's an example: Fischer & Wieser makes jams, jellies, and sauces. They raised the price of one of their products from $1.95 to $1.99—just four cents. With this increase, in one year, they were able to increase their profitability by $40,000. A tiny change allowed them to realize a meaningful profit lift.

---

their goals to the company strategy, and they feel more connected to the company's success. This transparency not only motivates them but also builds trust. They'll see how their efforts contribute directly to the bottom line, fostering a stronger team spirit and driving everyone to work together toward common goals. It's about creating an environment where everyone is pulling in the same direction.

As humans, we think in round numbers. We know from numerous studies in behavioral economics, psychology, and neuroscience that it's our nature to find patterns and make approximations. For example, a 2020 study by a behavioral economist found that we are wired to prefer round numbers, even if an irregular number would save us money. This effect shows up in business when deciding what price to charge, how much margin to target, or how big of a price increase to implement. Your profit picture will be transformed, however, if your team asks themselves some questions to disrupt that thinking:

- What percent increase can we do without sacrificing sales volume? If it's not 5 percent, could it be 3 percent? Or 2? Or 0.5 percent?
- If a certain margin target is too high to remain competitive for a certain customer opportunity, what is the highest margin we can charge? For example, if a 30 percent margin isn't realistic, don't drop all the way to 25 percent if 28 percent can still win you the business.
- If there are some areas of our business with zero opportunity to get even a fraction of a percent more, are there other parts of our business where we can? Are there *any* products, services, customers, or opportunities where we can get 5, 3, 2, or 0.5 percent?

The answer to this last question, in even the most competitive and commoditized industries, is yes, at least for some of your products and services to some of your customers. There are places hiding out in your business where you have this kind of opportunity. And for every business, no matter their financial performance, a small price change has the power to revolutionize their profit picture.

Tiny price changes make a huge difference.

"It's Easier to Grow Profits by Selling More"

Most companies I encounter are extremely focused on growing sales volume as a way to increase profits. Of course, I support growing sales volume. Definitely, sell more. But to meaningfully drive profit lift through sales growth alone, generally, means a lot of hard work.

Earlier in the chapter, I showed how a 5 percent price increase doubled the bottom-line profit of a company. To double your bottom line through sales growth alone, you have to sell *So. Much. More.* And, just as difficult, now you also have to meet all that demand you just sold. You have to manufacture, pack, and ship more products—or, if you work in a service business, you have to do more engineering or marketing or legal services. Regardless of what you sell, it takes a lot more labor to double sales and fulfill the work. (At the time of writing this book, the labor market was extremely tight, and recruiting and retaining people was difficult and costly. Even with a looser labor market, finding, hiring, and keeping top talent isn't easy or cheap.) It means more quotes, proposals, and designs. It means more orders, more invoices, and more chasing down customers who don't pay on time. It means ensuring that the quality of your products and services doesn't slip in the process of doing more to sell more. Sometimes, in all the rush, it's easier to make expensive mistakes. And then you have to fix those mistakes, expedite materials, work overtime—all of which pushes costs up.

I'm not suggesting volume growth isn't a good thing. I'm simply pointing out that it creates cost and work to execute—and almost always, a faster, easier way to increase profits is with pricing. (Best case scenario: Do both. Despite what you learned in economics class, it's possible to raise prices and sell more through surgical and strategic price management, as you'll learn in this book.)

How much more do you have to deliver when you raise prices? Zero. No extra orders, no extra shipments, no extra projects, no overtime hours, no additional employees to meet demand... and you get paid what your product or service is worth.

The myth that the best way to grow profits is by selling more is a costly one. We've all heard that "sales cure all ills" and that selling more creates extra wiggle room and generates more money that can be used for any business challenges. While there is truth to that statement, it ignores how hard it is to grow volume substantially and serve it compared with how easy it is, relatively speaking, to generate that same profit lift with modest changes in price.

And another thing: Profit is the funding engine for the future, growth, and sustainability of your company. Many businesses are too narrowly focused on revenue and volume growth. Remember: You don't make investments in your business based on revenue. Your investments

> **The myth that the best way to grow profits is by selling more is a costly one.**

in growth, your team, new products, and so on are funded from the pool of profits. It's not what's going on at the top line that informs your ability to invest—it's the bottom line.

In other words, you aren't robbing 1 or 2 or 5 percent of your business' future when you underprice. You're robbing 20 or 40 or 100 percent. I heard a phrase years ago from a CEO that I love and often repeat:

Revenue is for vanity. Profit is for sanity.

Every single percentage point of price has a huge impact on the bottom line. Give some of the time, attention, and urgency to pricing that you have given to volume growth, and watch your profits rise as a result.

"We Know This Math Already!"

At this point, I have not blown your mind. You aren't dropping the book to run off and call your sales manager to tell her the mind-bending power of 1 percent. You already understand how powerful a 1 percent price change is. You've heard it, you've witnessed it, and you've told your team about it.

Here's the thing: it's not about knowing the math. I'll say that again: *it's not about knowing the math.* It's about *living* the math every day, for every deal, every product, every service, every customer. Every. Single. Time.

Are you and everyone who sells on your behalf *consistently excellent* at this? Do you look for every single chance to make sure you're maximizing the extra percent? Do you seek to maximize every fraction of a point of price on every single deal?

The answer to that question, in my experience, is no. Not every member of your team is consistently excellent at it. And I realize many things work against perfection in pricing. Your people are running as fast as they can. Every company is doing more with less. Pricing is a minute part of a salesperson's job when they have a thousand other priorities to manage. Sometimes, pulling costing together takes hours or days or weeks, and a pricing decision gets made ten minutes before the bid is due. Without question, there are obstacles to consistent excellence.

But I invite you to consider that *you don't have to be perfect at this.* Could you get infinitesimally better at it? If you can improve by a fraction—if you can pick up 0.5 percent or even

1 percent—it could mean double-digit profit growth. Can you get just a little bit better? It's not about knowing the math. It's about living with it tattooed on the back of your eyelids. It's about feeling the gut-wrenching frustration of leaked profit every time you miss a chance to do it.

From my time on keynote stages, I know that most businesses believe they're already doing everything possible to maximize pricing. Here is an exercise to help you identify if your sales team is really taking advantage of the pricing pulley in your business.

Ask each member of your sales team to bring to you their last ten deals. Then ask: "In your best judgment, if the price of this opportunity had been 1 percent higher, would we still have won the deal?" Sort the deals into two piles:

NO: Increasing the price of this deal by 1 percent most likely would have lost the deal.

YES: Increasing the price of this deal by 1 percent would most likely not have jeopardized it. It's likely we could have increased the price by 1 percent and the customer would have still said yes.

How many deals ended up in the NO pile? How many in the YES pile?

When we do this exercise with companies, they often find that all but one or two deals, and sometimes every deal, is in the YES pile. I then ask them to tally up the total of the 1 percent price lift on the YES deals. One team from a large HVAC manufacturer's rep firm found that those 1 percent increases totaled $500,000.

What are some things *your* company could do with that kind of money?

Are you maximizing your opportunities to gain every penny of price for every deal, every customer, every product, every service?

The sales manager for the HVAC company was shocked by how easy it was to maximize pricing in this way because *he was sure they were already doing it.* Like this company, your business may be maximizing many of your opportunities to gain every penny of price. But are you doing it every time—for every deal, every customer, every product, every service?

One percent typically isn't a lot to ask for, but it adds up fast.

Most business leaders know and understand the power of a 1 percent price increase, but unless they are doing it rigorously and consistently, they are not maximizing price for the value they deliver to every customer on every product and service on every deal.

Get In the Reps!

I know you know this stuff. But *knowing* and *doing* are two different things. And not only doing, but doing consistently, rigorously, with excellence, with perfect form.

Here's a simple example: I learned to do push-ups when I was perhaps five or six years old. I've known how to do a push-up for decades—for most of my life.

But if you were to watch me do a push-up, I am certain you could critique my form. You would see *something* I'm not doing perfectly.

It's not just about knowing to do something or even knowing how to do it. It's about doing it repeatedly, consistently, effectively, and with excellent form. Get in the reps!

The Pricing Pulley Exercise

To see how the pricing pulley will benefit your business, complete the Pricing Pulley worksheet with your sales team.

1. Ask them to think through the customers and deals they've won over the past month.
2. Which of those deals could they have won even with a price that was 1 percent higher? (While they can't know this for sure, they can make their best educated guess).
3. Have them record those deals on the Pricing Pulley worksheet.
4. They can calculate what that 1 percent of revenue represents for those deals within the last month.
5. Annualize the number by multiplying by 12.
6. Add it all together to see how much price and profit you left on the table.
7. Finally, have them brainstorm the areas where they would invest that money for company growth—to be a better place to work, to help them do their jobs better, to attract and serve customers better, etc.

WORKSHEET | PRICING PULLEY

DEAL #1

DEAL #2

DEAL #3

DEAL #4

TOTAL ADDITIONAL REVENUE

INVESTMENT IDEAS

Here's an example of the worksheet completed by one of our clients, a commercial construction company:

WORKSHEET | PRICING PULLEY

DEAL #1	DEAL DESCRIPTION	Riverdale Tech Hub Dev
	DEAL REVENUE	$2,000,000
	1% OF REVENUE	$20,000

DEAL #2	DEAL DESCRIPTION	Maple Grove Warehouse
	DEAL REVENUE	$1,500,000
	1% OF REVENUE	$15,000

DEAL #3	DEAL DESCRIPTION	Evergreen Plaza Reno
	DEAL REVENUE	$3,000,000
	1% OF REVENUE	$30,000

DEAL #4	DEAL DESCRIPTION	LSA Parking Expansion
	DEAL REVENUE	$800,000
	1% OF REVENUE	$8,000

TOTAL ADDITIONAL REVENUE	$73,000

INVESTMENT IDEAS	
Site Survey Drones	Raises & Bonuses
More Advertising	Hire More PMs
LEED Accreditation	Computer Training
New CRM	Buy New Telehandler
Buy New Safety Gear	Community Projects
Buy 3D Printer	Hire More Estimators

Download a fillable PDF of the Pricing Pulley Worksheet here:

An Invitation

In my experience, there is often a disconnect between knowing the math behind the power of 1 percent and applying it to every single deal, every single customer, and every single product or service. Is every single person who prices and sells on behalf of your company selling as if the future of your business is at stake? Are they—are you—seizing every opportunity to maximize pricing?

I invite you to find those places where you can increase prices by 1 or 5 percent or even a fraction of a percent, to apply the pricing pulley principle when negotiating every deal with every customer.

Just as important as finding where you can raise prices is finding where you concede price by discounting. If small increases lift profits, discounts kill them. In the next chapter, we'll look at discounting practices and ask whether discounts are necessary to win business. Often, the answer is no.

Key Takeaways

- A minimal price increase (as small as 1 percent, or even smaller) can result in a significant boost in profitability.
- Many businesses overlook the profit-lifting potential of pricing, focusing more on sales growth or cost reduction.
- Small adjustments in pricing can substantially impact your profitability without increasing operational workload.
- Applying the "pulley effect" of pricing requires consistent and rigorous application across all sales and customer interactions.
- The concept of a pricing pulley should be a key part of a company's pricing strategy and execution.

Client Spotlight: Beka Eisenbarth, H-P Products

Some business is worth letting go. And sometimes when you let it go, it comes back.

That was the lesson learned at H-P Products, where Beka Eisenbarth had recently taken over the reins of the company her grandfather founded in 1948. She was following in the footsteps of her grandmother, H-P's first female president, and succeeding a president whose focus had always been on operations—on cutting costs and producing more. This was 2022: inflation was taking off, costs were going up, and everyone was rationing. And Eisenbarth wanted to raise prices.

"We were a very operational-focused company," Eisenbarth says about the years before she became president of H-P, whose business is tubular fabrications and central vacuum systems. "We cared about getting more done, and more out than we did on the top line in pricing. It wasn't our past president's focus at all. In fact, I never heard him talk about pricing."

But Eisenbarth saw an opportunity. When she became president, one of the first things she did was bring Boost in to work with H-P's sales team on pricing.

"Casey reminds [you] that you are excellent—get paid for it," Eisenbarth says. "She's right; we are excellent. On every metric, when we ask our customers, they all say we're excellent. But we weren't making it financially. It didn't make sense. It actually got to a point where I said, 'If we can't make money at what we're doing today, we have to pivot.'"

Eisenbarth decided to raise prices—and not just by a little. She raised them by around 40 percent. "It terrified my sales team," she says. And they weren't the only ones who felt apprehensive. "I sound like I'm so confident, but I had some sleepless nights."

The first thing that happened was that customers started calling. Her salespeople came to her worried: "'This customer is really mad.' I said, 'Okay, did they place the order? Did they move their business?' And they said, 'No, no, they need it.'" And when the customers were really angry, she told her sales team, "Let's talk to them. Let's have empathy. This isn't a dictatorship; I want customers for life. Let's explain our why and the value we're bringing to the table."

It was more work for the sales team in the beginning—to explain the price increase, defend it, and give their whys. Together with Boost, Eisenbarth worked on training her team on the messaging for their customers, and her salespeople started to see results. "They would come to me and say, 'Now [the customers] are starting to settle down, and they see it—they realize we have material our competitors don't, and if they want their lines to stay up, they'll have to pay for it.'"

In some cases, customers left H-P after the price increase. Eisenbarth says they had to have the courage to let that happen. Sometimes, customers left for good, but sometimes, they came back more loyal than ever.

"I had a customer come back," Eisenbarth recalls. "He said to me, 'Listen, I tried the other guy. I had to—your prices went up so much.' I told him, 'I understand. You have a job too.' He said, 'But nobody can do what you guys can do.' I said, 'I know. It's really hard to do what we're doing. That's why I think we should get paid for it.' He said, 'I know—I won't do it again.'"

When customers didn't come back, it was another transformative exercise for the sales team. They learned that sometimes it's okay to let a piece of business go. "What a dramatic message that was," she says. They knew they were getting paid what they were worth, and as for the customers who left and stayed gone, she told her salespeople, "We are worth more than this. If they can't value your talents, time, and treasure, let's find someone who will. We know there are plenty of people out there. Let's go find them.' I mean, that's part of being able to sell. You want to feel proud of what you're standing behind and that someone values it as much as you value it. We say every year that we pick who we do business with. We're very fortunate that we are able to choose, and not everybody should be chosen."

The significant price increase, while creating more work initially, has led to a cultural shift at H-P. When the focus was on producing more and cutting costs, the burden was placed firmly on the production team. They had to work harder for the company to make more money. Now, Eisenbarth says, "we've never had happier employees. It's a lot easier to raise prices half a percent than try to eke that half percent out of production."

H-P had a record year of profitability even with lower volumes. The sales team is still adjusting to only taking business that makes sense for them to take. "It's working right now," she says. "We have some capacity. But it's got to be the right thing to add to this funnel. We've never had an easier time making money. I think more is not better.

"I showed them that you can work less for more just through pricing."

Eisenbarth looks at the business both before and after the price increase and sees "two different worlds." Improving pricing generated a seven-figure improvement to profits. When customers pushed back, she encouraged her salespeople to stick with it. "I said, 'Maintain our deliveries, maintain our quality, make sure we're doing all the things we said we're going to do.' And it's been transformative to our profitability. There's just no other way to say it."

CHAPTER 2

DISCOUNTS KILL PROFITS

Learning Objectives

1. Examine the negative impact of discounting on profit margins.
2. Challenge the myth of "making it up in volume."
3. Resist unnecessary discounting.

Even small discounts can kill your profit.

If a small price increase has a large positive effect on your profitability, a small discount on price has a large *negative* effect on your profitability.

In the last chapter, we saw what a 1, 2, 5, and 10 percent price increase would translate to in bottom-line profit for your business. That pulley effect works the same way with discounts.

If you have a 5 percent bottom-line profit:

- 1% discount = 20% reduction in bottom-line profit
- 2% discount = 40% reduction in bottom-line profit
- 5% discount = 100% reduction in bottom-line profit

Let's explore how this works using the "world's simplest P&L" example company from the last chapter. With a 5 percent discount, every dollar of revenue drops to $0.95. The expense line doesn't change, since it doesn't cost any less to produce or distribute your product or provide your service when you discount. The bottom line goes from $0.05 to $0.00. Zero. As in, no profit. A 5 percent discount just wiped out your entire net profit.

"Just" a 5% Price Discount Costs 100% Profit

 **REVENUE** $0.95

 **- COST** $0.95

  PROFIT $0.00

As in the price increase example, we see a 20X impact here: for every percent you discount the price, you decrease your bottom-line profit by 20 percent. Remember this magnification effect the next time you consider offering "just a 5 percent discount" to a customer. Never offer discounts without knowing how much profitability the discount will eat up. Guard every percent of price like gold because it *is* gold.

Never offer discounts without knowing how much profitability the discount will eat up. Guard every percent of price like gold because it *is* gold.

"Make It Up in Volume"

One of the most common myths I hear from sales teams regarding discounting is that they will "make it up in volume." I cannot calculate how many extra widgets you have to sell at *zero* net profit to be money ahead.

When we price aggressively to "make it up in volume," what happens to profitability? It's gutted. You are busy, busy, busy making no money. Every business owner in the world knows this is an exhausting, miserable, demoralizing, soul-sucking experience, and you're too good at what you do to be this kind of company.

Consider two important things about the idea of making it up in volume:

1. **The increased volume often doesn't justify the requested discount.** I see this over and over again. For example, a company making 30 percent gross margin requires a 50 percent increase in sales volume *just to break even* with a 10 percent discount. (See Figure 2.1.) Anything less than 50 percent sales

volume growth, and they'll lose money in the bargain. Gaining volume and making less money means going home tired *and* hungry.

2. **Sales teams notoriously overestimate the volume they will gain at discounted prices.** (That's because sales teams and other internal price setters overestimate price elasticity. More on that in Part 3.) If you discount to gain volume, understand the financial impact first. In addition, how is your sales team's say/do ratio regarding sales growth with discounts? If it's not so hot, use that information to combat future requests for discounts.

One other costly thing to keep in mind: if you're discounting under the old "make it up in volume" idea, you might frequently find that you're expediting materials, working overtime, and sometimes making expensive mistakes, turning this endeavor into a loss rather than a gain pretty quickly.

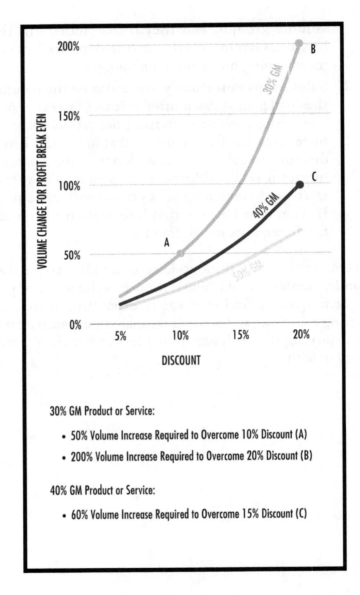

Figure 2.1 Volume change to break even on gross margin by percentage price change

For more on the relationship between price and volume, including helpful tools, see the section "How to Make Data-Driven Decisions" in Chapter 3 and the tools in Part 5.

What Happens When You Discount

When I talk to business leaders about discounting, the response I often hear is, "But sometimes we *have* to discount."

I acknowledge that discounting is sometimes necessary in business. There are customers who will walk away because of price, and there are times when you have to discount in light of the commercial and competitive situation. But I challenge you to consider that you often discount when you shouldn't.

Would you believe me if I told you that, sometimes, you are discounting to customers who have already decided to buy from you? You are the one they want. You are the only one who can get it done on time. You are the only one they trust to deliver on their creative vision or their technical vision. You are the only one who has the part in stock. You may even be the lowest price. They have already decided to buy from you. They just haven't told you yet. They start putting pressure on you to see if they can get it for less. These folks are in what I affectionately call the "Can't Hurt to Ask Club."

Here's an example of how this goes, which I bet everyone reading this book has experienced:

> A customer approaches you and says, "What does it cost for this collection of products/services?" You quote them a price—let's say it's $42,000—and then you tell them all the reasons it's a smart investment, all the

great results they can expect, and other value-selling points. The customer says, "You know, I'd really love to work with you, but I have several other quotes sitting on my desk that are significantly lower. You don't have to be the lowest, but you have to be in the ballpark. If there's any way you could do this for $39,000, I'd love to go with you. Can you make that happen? Thanks so much."

What do you believe when the customer tells you they need a discount to say yes? You start thinking it's true. *Can I do it for $39,000? It's still a pretty decent margin. One hundred percent of $39,000 is better than zero percent of $42,000. We're having a soft month, and I really could use this sale. Not only that, but I've been trying to get my foot in the door with this customer forever. I can make up this discount on future volume…* You start to believe that this discount is the only way you're going to win the deal, and discounting is better than losing it.

Here is what is going on in the mind of this customer: *I did get several other quotes. Somebody quoted $22,000— they screwed up or missed something in the scope. I got one quote at $49,000—it's a Cadillac quote, full of stuff I'd love but don't need. It's over-scoped for my needs and budget. And I got one at $39,000, but I know from other people in my department that the company has been late before, causing a ton of problems, and I can't deal with that. As long as this* [your] *quote comes in anywhere south of $45,000, I'll go with them* [you]. *And I'm going to use the $39,000 quote to see if I can get them* [you] *to drop their* [your] *price.*

They are already planning to buy from you. Your price already fell inside an acceptable range, but you are ready to discount because they said they need it for less. You will get the work either way, but you are victim to the "Can't Hurt to Ask" buying tactic, and it costs you substantial profit.

Customers in the "Can't Hurt to Ask Club" are doing what humans do—fishing for a better price. Have you ever tried this tactic yourself? Has it ever worked? Were you prepared to pay the higher price even if they said no to the discount? Yes, yes, and yes. We *all* do this as buyers, but we completely forget that when we sell. It seems so simple and so obvious, but we forget it, and it's costing our companies significant money.

"Can't Hurt to Ask" happens in every single industry. It happens in B2B, B2C, B2G, and nonprofit. It happens on tiny deals and enormous deals. It happens whether you sell goods or services. It happens everywhere in the capitalist economy *because it works*. It costs your customers nothing to try it; that's why I call it the Can't Hurt to Ask Club!

Believing the Illusions

The customer's "Can't Hurt to Ask" tactic works because you fall prey to two illusions they project.

The first illusion: The customer projects a volume threat that doesn't exist. They are going to buy from you. But you believe there is a volume threat. It makes you afraid, and you discount out of fear.

A customer projecting a volume threat for discounts can sound quite innocuous. They may ask, "Is that your best number?" Or "Is there anything you could do to help me out?" Or "Can you sharpen your pencil?" Sometimes, it's a bit more direct, with customers giving you the so-called last look. And sometimes, it can be far more aggressive, where they may even flat-out lie about their intention to buy from someone else to get you to lower your price. I've even seen customers set up a bid process when they already know who they plan to buy from. They use the bidding environment to put pressure on their intended vendor.

Phantom volume threats are a powerful buyer's tool to undercut your value.

And often, even when that vendor doesn't bid the lowest price, the customer plucks them out of the middle of the price range and awards the business to them anyway. Phantom volume threats are a powerful buyer's tool to undercut your value. Don't let them do it.

Sometimes, when we present this customer tactic to sales teams in our training programs, they object, particularly in industries where there are deep, long-standing relationships with customers. They don't want to believe that their customers would exploit their fear and lack of confidence. They insist they have a true partnership, and their customers would never do something like this. I've heard *I've been selling to Bill for 32 years. I had dinner with him and his wife last week. Bill wouldn't do this to me.* Yes, Bill would. Yes, Bill does. It is Bill's job to do it to you. It's not personal. It doesn't make Bill a jerk. It doesn't mean Bill doesn't respect you and value your products and services. It's just that Bill has a boss to answer to or a team of employees to afford. It's his job to do this.

Your customers are not jerks, crooks, or bad people for projecting phantom volume threats, just as you're not when you use this maneuver as a buyer. It's your customer's job to get what you sell for less than it's worth. It's your job to get paid well for the value you offer. That causes the natural tension of sales. It's not personal.

The second illusion: The customer has all the power. They're handing out orders and contracts; they're making deals and writing checks. You're trying like heck to be their choice, and you buy into the illusion that the customer has all the power and you have none.

When you sell that way, you sell from fear. And selling from fear causes you to underprice and overdiscount.

But that isn't the real power dynamic. The true dynamic is more balanced. When you recognize that, you don't sell from fear. You sell from confidence.

The customer may always have a little bit of an upper hand, but I invite you to con-sider that the power split is much more balanced than you believe. Why? Because

> **Selling from fear causes you to underprice and overdiscount.**

the customer *needs* what you sell. They need your services. They need your products. They are going to buy from someone. Why not from you?

If you believe in what you sell, if you solve a real problem for people and do it with value, excellence, and quality, then you hold some of the power. So, sell from confidence. You'll do far less fear-based discounting and selling.

Prediscounting

The discounting of which we're most aware happens after we propose a price to a customer, that is, when they beat us up on price, object, or compare us to a competitor's quote. Those are the kinds of discounts we often talk about in sales meetings and we measure and seek to reduce.

But, sometimes, we discount before the customer even sees the price. I call this sneaky form of discounting "pre-discounting." This happens when we talk ourselves out of the right price before we ever present it to the customer. We don't give them a chance to beat us up—we do it to ourselves.

This happens because we lack confidence and act out of fear—because we buy into the illusion that the customer has all the power, or we're stung by the last deal we lost. We think *The customer will never go for that.* We give ourselves sticker shock over our own price.

So, we knock down the number before we propose it to the customer: *$250,000? I think their budget is probably closer to $225,000. I'm going to bid $225,000.* Whatever the discount looks like, whether it's 2 or 10 percent, we have convinced ourselves that this is what we need to do to win the deal. And the customer hasn't even joined the conversation yet.

A client in a professional services industry told me, "We never discount without changing scope. If we change price for a customer, we remove something from the project." They figure out who from their team will work on the project and how many hours, days, and weeks each person will need to complete the job. Then, they apply the standard rates from their price schedule for each team member to calculate an overall fixed-fee price for the project—a common cost-plus approach to a professional services project.

I may be skeptical, but it's rare to have that kind of discipline and price integrity, so I asked if they ever looked at a price they'd calculated for a project before presenting it to the customer and worried it was too high. Had they ever experienced that internal sticker shock and started slashing hours from a project until it felt "acceptable?"

Sheepishly, the client admitted that yes, sometimes they did that. Then, problematically, their profits suffered in delivery because they would put in the time required to make the project a success for their customer—as originally calculated! The project would come in over budgeted hours and under profit because their internal sticker shock made them slash much-needed hours.

I've seen prediscounting in every industry, regardless of whether you sell products or services. Don't talk yourself out of the price you deserve. Don't discount yourself before you even quote the customer. Let the customer be the one to beat you up (and be ready to defend your price). Don't negotiate against yourself!

How can your salespeople interrupt their own thinking to avoid prediscounting?

Don't talk yourself out of the price you deserve.

1. **Pay attention to it.** Acknowledge that your own beliefs, fears, and worries about what the customer will say or losing the deal will stop you from asking for a fair and competitive price.

2. **Interrogate whether you might be prediscounting and to what degree.** The next time you're putting together pricing, and you arrive at an initial price but then decide to knock it down a bit, have a serious conversation with yourself—or, even better, with a manager or a colleague—and defend that number.

   If it's a dollar a pound, why couldn't it be $1.05? Spend five minutes convincing yourself or your manager that there is no chance it could be $1.05. Or, if it's a $10,000 project, there's no chance it could be $10,500. Why couldn't it be? Why would it never be competitive for this particular opportunity?

Have a detailed conversation about this opportunity and look objectively at the factors that drive your decision-making. What are the commercial and competitive realities? What is the competitive density? What is the complexity of the opportunity? Who is the customer, and how does your relationship with them factor in?

If your argument against a higher price is weak or thin, you may be prediscounting. Don't miss an opportunity to get a little more for what you're offering.

Get Granular in Your Thinking

We've been talking about when and why we discount: We buy into the myths our customers project, and we act out of fear. We anticipate their objections, and we reduce the price before they've seen our quote.

Do we discount too readily and too often? Probably. Is discounting always a mistake? No.

It would be commercially and competitively unrealistic for me to say that discounting is never the right move. But when faced with a situation where a discount is necessary, ask yourself if that discount can be smaller.

Do you have to go all the way down to 5 percent off? Do you have to match your competitor's price? Do you have to go to $39,000, like in the previous example, or can you go part way? Anything you can do to shorten up your discounts, even by a fraction of a percent, will make a massive difference for your

> **If a discount is necessary, ask yourself if the discount can be smaller.**

profitability. If 1 percent of my price cost me 20 percent of my profitability, I'd be fighting hard to hold on to even a fraction of a percent.

Our brains naturally want to go with round numbers: 5 percent off, 10 percent off, $1,000 or $2,000 off. But what about 2 or 4 percent off? Instead of $1,000 off, what about $500, $250, or $47 off? If you're a cost-plus organization, instead of thinking, "We probably can't get a 30 percent margin on this job, so let's do 25," what about 28 percent?

In Chapter 1, we talked about how price increases don't have to be executed in big round chunks. They can be small; they can be fractional. I know it has been a long time since fourth grade, but do yourself a favor and reintroduce your brain to **fractions** and **decimals**! Instead of 28 percent margin, what about 28.2 percent? Every one of us walks around all day with a calculator in our pockets—our cell phone. Don't let failure to do a simple calculation be the reason you don't make more money.

Getting more granular in your thinking with pricing will vastly improve your profitability. Just because our brains are lazy and think in big chunks is not a good reason to forgo profit.

Mark It Up to Mark It Down

One question I am frequently asked after keynote presentations is, "What about the 'mark it up to mark it down' approach?" This is when companies inflate their initial price so they can discount it when they get price pressure from customers. The idea is that the final, "marked down" price is high enough for you, and the customer is still happy.

To me, this is a pricing game, and I am not, generally, a big fan of pricing games. It reminds me of shopping at Kohl's. Everything is on sale at Kohl's—*everything*. When I check out, the receipt tells me that I "saved $287 by shopping at Kohl's today!" But I bought a tank top and a candle, and I'm on to you, Kohl's! This doesn't feel like a deal. They marked everything up just so they could put it on sale and try to make me feel good about it.

The "mark it up to mark it down" strategy in B2B price negotiations tends to work in the same way: both sides know it's a game, and the customer wonders if they left money on the table and fears they've been fleeced. It can create a dangerous pattern of negotiating with customers. For this reason, my general rule is *don't play pricing games*.

Here's the exception to the general rule: Don't play pricing games *unless you must*. It's important to understand the landscape in which you operate. In some industries and geographies, pricing games such as these are standard, and you will be at a competitive disadvantage if you don't play them. Also, some purchasing agents are awarded bonuses and promoted based on their ability to get discounts from you, so pricing games in those situations can occasionally be appropriate, even if a bit distasteful. If you decide to play the "mark it up to mark it down" game, I recommend two important guidelines:

- **Know the "rules of the game."** If the purchasing agent is compensated based on discount versus initial price, the "mark it up to mark it down" game can be a sound strategy, as the absolute price matters less than the relative price. The buyer gets to be the hero for negotiating a 10 percent discount from you. Sometimes, especially where you have a good relationship, buyers will even show you their hand in a way that allows for a win-win. Ask, "On what are you being measured?" If they say, for example, "I don't have any room on unit pricing, but I have some flexibility around freight," you know where you need to sharpen your pencil and where to pad more price in.

- **Consider building in easy "givebacks."** What are the elements of the deal that can be easily descoped as you mark down the price? If you know you are going to be in for a tough price negotiation, having some products, services, or features that you can pull out as you mark down is a nice way to maintain price integrity.

Key Takeaways

- Even small discounts can have a disproportionately large negative impact on profits.
- The belief that lost profits from discounts can be recouped through increased sales volume is often misguided.
- Understanding the full financial impact of discounting helps in making more informed pricing decisions.
- Companies should be wary of customer tactics like the projection of volume threats to secure discounts.

- There's often more pricing opportunity than sellers realize, even in competitive markets.
- Pricing decisions should be data-driven, not fear-driven.
- Sales teams need confidence in their pricing and the value they offer.

Client Spotlight: Bob Domnick, Superior Industries

When Superior Industries, a leading manufacturer of bulk material processing equipment, found itself confronting unpredictable market shifts due to geopolitical conflicts and rising steel costs, CEO Bob Domnick saw his sales team struggle to meet their pricing goals while competing with lower-priced competitors. The company faced significant challenges in maintaining profitability while navigating a number of price increases.

Domnick brought in the Boost team to conduct a training program for Superior involving 75 employees, primarily sales and management. The program was centered on establishing and strengthening strategies for better pricing execution.

"This was a time when we had a project in Russia we had to just cancel and get out of [because of the war in Ukraine], and the price of steel was out of whack, so we had to deliver a total of seven price increases through that run-up," Domnick recalls. The sales team "knew, during the price escalation, that we had to come on strong if we were going to survive."

Over the course of the ten-week training program, the participating sales and management teams focused on four main objectives:

- **Identifying services and value-adds they were giving away for free.** For example, the construction management team had never charged for project-management services when building out turnkey systems. In a small-group discussion during training, one salesperson suggested charging a fee for project management, which resulted in an additional $100,000 on one $6 million project.

- **Understanding the power of 1 percent.** The training illustrated the immense potential of a 1 percent price increase and involved the team in a discussion about where to reinvest that lift back into the business. Helping the team see how essential protecting price was to the future and sustainability of the enterprise helped to align their actions to the interests of the company.

- **Tailoring pricing based on volume and customer needs.** Instead of applying blanket, round-number discounts, the team learned how to get granular with pricing. "If there's a large volume order, and you're going to give a discount, it doesn't have to be 5 percent. It can be 4 percent; it can be 3.5 percent," Domnick says. This approach helped them maintain healthy margins while negotiating deals effectively.

- **Building confidence in their services and offerings.** The training instilled a sense of pride in the team, leading to stronger negotiations with clients and empowering them to stand firm on pricing unless there was a corresponding reduction in the offering.

By implementing these facets of the pricing discipline in their daily sales operations, the company was able to withstand market volatility while also driving substantial profit growth, Domnick says. "We have competitors lowering pricing, and even my sales team is not coming to me to lower prices. It's just that powerful."

CHAPTER 3

PRICE-VOLUME RELATIONSHIP

Learning Objectives

1. Explore the relationship between price changes, sales volume, and profitability.
2. Analyze the implications of potential sales volume loss due to price increases.
3. Equip sales teams with skills to make data-driven pricing decisions.

We've explored how small price increases generate a significant lift on profits and how small discounts kill them. Having worked with business leaders and sales teams for many years, I know that understanding these principles is not the same thing as executing on them every deal.

Before we look at other ways customers try to get more from you for less and how you can combat that, I want to address a fear among sales teams—they will lose volume if they increase price.

Let me start by saying that I am not okay with losing sales volume. I'm not saying that you should raise prices and not worry about losing customers because it's all about being more profitable at the end of the day. My goal is for you to raise prices *and* keep your customers through strategic and surgical application of this book's principles.

I know, however, that analyzing what happens when you raise prices—whether you lose volume or not—is critical for helping you make data-driven, not fear-based, decisions about pricing in your business. If the worst happens, what will your profit picture look like? I want to show you that you can bind the risk and the fear to give you the starch in the back to raise prices.

Let's start with my client, a manufacturing company in Cincinnati. I'll call them Apex Industries. This company operates with a 20 percent gross margin and a 5 percent net margin. Just like the example company in the first two chapters, Apex's 5 percent net profit means that a 1 percent price increase would give a 20 percent lift in profitability. A 5 percent increase would double their profitability, as shown in Figure 3.1.

Make data-driven decisions, not fear-driven decisions.

METRIC	BASE CASE	PRICE CHANGE	VOLUME CHANGE	IMPACT TO PROFIT
Revenue	$30,000,000	5.0%	0.0%	100.0%
Gross Margin	$6,000,000			$1,500,000
Net Profit	$1,500,000			

Figure 3.1 Sample scenario showing profit
impact of a 5 percent price increase

The visual in Figure 3.1 is taken from a simplified version of the Profitability Levers Model explained in Chapter 16. Using this simple calculator, you can run "what-if" scenarios with changes in price and volume to understand the profit impact. This model will help you understand the true impact of discounts, and it's extremely useful to combat the seductive sales myth of "making it up in volume."

Download the Profitability Levers Model here:

When I went through that math using the world's simplest P&L with the sales team, they were quick to object: "Sure, we can raise prices. But won't we lose volume?"

"Okay," I said. "How much sales volume do you think you'll lose?"

They said, "Not sure. It could be 5 percent. Maybe more. Could be close to 10 percent!" I asked if 8 percent was fair, and they said it was. As you can see in Figure 3.2, gaining 5 percent in price with an 8 percent volume loss still netted this company $900,000 incremental profit, representing 60 percent growth to their bottom line:

METRIC	BASE CASE	PRICE CHANGE	VOLUME CHANGE	IMPACT TO PROFIT
Revenue	$30,000,000	5.0%	-8.0%	60.0%
Gross Margin	$6,000,000			$900,000
Net Profit	$1,500,000			

Figure 3.2 Sample scenario showing profit impact of a
5 percent price increase with 8 percent volume loss

This analysis makes it clear that Apex should proceed
with a 5 percent price increase even with a volume loss of
8 percent. The result would be *higher* profits. However, in
all my years of working with sales teams, I have never seen
a sales team accurately predict sales volume loss from a
price increase. They always overestimate sales volume loss
from price actions.

Much as we anticipate sticker shock on behalf of our
customers before we even present a quote, we also overestimate our customers' response to a price increase. We are
more price-sensitive on behalf of our customers than our

customers are. So, I'd guess Apex's sales volume loss will not be 8 percent. It'll be 6 or 4 percent—or even zero.

I gave the Apex sales team the benefit of the doubt that they were mostly right about volume loss with a price increase, so I did the next calculation at 6 percent volume loss. With a 6 percent volume loss, Apex would still be 70 percent more profitable after the price increase, with over a million dollars of incremental bottom-line profit:

> **I have never seen a sales team accurately predict sales volume loss from a price increase. They always overestimate sales volume loss from price actions.**

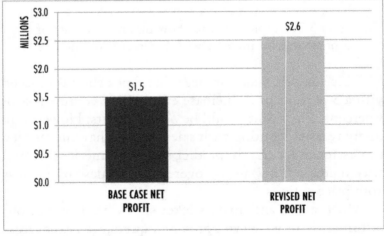

METRIC	BASE CASE	PRICE CHANGE	VOLUME CHANGE	IMPACT TO PROFIT
Revenue	$30,000,000	5.0%	-6.0%	70.0%
Gross Margin	$6,000,000			$1,050,000
Net Profit	$1,500,000			

Figure 3.3 Sample scenario showing profit impact of a 5 percent price increase with 6 percent volume loss

The math takes (some of) the emotion out of it. A 5 percent price increase is a no-brainer for Apex.

Is Our Estimate of Volume Loss Correct?

Very few companies actually model out a price increase with specific volume-loss assumptions. In other words, they hesitate to enact price increases and/or enact smaller price increases out of an *unspecified* volume loss. This results in making a fear-driven decision rather than a data-driven decision. They are afraid of the monster under the bed, but they have no idea if the monster has sharp claws or is a fluffy bunny.

Shine a light under the bed. Calculate the impact. Often, you'll find that even with a volume loss, profits are still significantly improved through a price increase. This type of analysis can bind your risk and fear, giving you the confidence to take action.

The sales team at Apex was more price-sensitive on behalf of their customers than their customers were, and so are your salespeople. You can't imagine how many times I've heard of companies wringing their hands and running calculations for months before a price increase, terrified of customer reaction, only to hear crickets. In other words, customers accepted the price increase without much fuss.

Why are sellers more price-sensitive than customers? When customers beat you up on price, your confidence begins to erode. That, of course, is what they want because if you aren't price-sensitive on their behalf, that's bad news for them. They will *never* tell you that your price is fair and reasonable. They *have to* push back. That's part of the social contract between buyers and sellers.

When I worked at General Electric, we would tell our sales teams first about a planned price increase. Without fail, the teams would immediately panic: *We can't raise prices, the customers will freak out, we'll lose volume, our competitors aren't raising prices...* Then, when we announced the price increase, the customers would also push back—but almost always with less force than the sales team did. And once the price change went into effect, the actual customer response was even lower—the actual volume loss was less than customers had threatened and much lower than sales reps had feared.

> The reason sellers have an inflated sense of price sensitivity is because buyers project an inflated sense of price sensitivity.

The reason sellers have an inflated sense of price sensitivity is because buyers project an inflated sense of price sensitivity. In other words, the disconnect between how loud customers complain and what they actually *do* is translated directly to a disconnect between what a salesperson believes about price sensitivity and the customer's actual price sensitivity.

My advice: don't spend your time planning around your sales teams' feelings over a price increase or your customers' reaction to it because they're almost always overinflated.

Don't Price to Keep Your Worst Customers

Citing sales volume loss as a reason not to raise prices creates another problem for your business. It means you're pricing to keep your worst customers. Let me explain.

Not all of the customers in the 6 percent are customers Apex is desperate to keep. Some of these customers are the *worst customers ever. Ever.* They don't value anything about what Apex offers that is unique.

Furthermore, this segment of customers is awful to do business with. They suck up disproportionate organizational resources. They abuse the company and their staff. They don't pay on time. They're not good customers, and Apex is going to make more money when they go away because there are costs to serve them that the company doesn't even realize exist. In short, Apex will be happy once they become Apex alumni.

Of course, some of this 6 percent includes good and valuable customers that Apex will be sorry to lose. Apex likes doing business with them. But have you ever lost a customer over price and had that customer return? They went looking for cheaper, and they found cheap? Not only are they back, but now they're no longer nearly as price-sensitive as they were when they left, and they're much more loyal. Presuming at least some of Apex's customers are like that, their net volume loss is not 6 percent—it's 5.8 or 5.2 or 4.9, or something lower.

Summing Up the Apex Example

It's important to understand the relationship between price and volume because we too easily write off a price increase out of fear of losing volume, and the Apex example shows that it's not a black-and-white proposition. The point is not to accept sales volume loss. The point is twofold:

1. When considering a price increase, do the math so that you're making an educated, data-driven decision versus a fear-driven decision.
2. Do not price to keep your worst customers because you will be underpricing.

Lies We Learned in Economics Class

"But if we raise prices, we'll lose volume." If I had a nickel for every time I've heard this from a business leader or salesperson, I'd have a castle of nickels. I'm about to take on the entire economics profession. Buckle up.

Economics teaches the law of demand:

- When price goes up, volume goes down.
- When price goes down, volume goes up.

Simple? Yes. A universal truth? Nope. But this so-called law is so entrenched in our systems, academics, literature, and psyches that the *Concise Encyclopedia of Economics* calls it the "most famous law in economics, and the one that economists are most sure of. On this law is built almost the whole edifice of economics."

Almost the whole edifice? Yikes.

This single economic axiom and its famous twin, the demand curve, have done more damage to pricing execution than any other economic principle.

I'm not saying the demand curve is a liar, but it definitely exaggerates.

Why do I find fault with the infatuation with the law of demand?

- There are many exceptions to the law of demand, as you can find in a two-minute Google search. I write about one of these, the Price-Quality Effect, in Chapter 10.

- The source of this law and the bulk of the research focuses on consumer goods, leaving out consumer services and the entire B2B world.

- This law rests on an important assumption—five beautiful, impossible words: "All other things being equal…"

This last one is the key to my objection. What, apart from price, must be held constant for this law to apply? All of them. This means:

- No changes in the preferences, needs, standards, goals, circumstances, budget, or behavior of individual buyers, nor in the collection of buyers as a whole market

- No differences whatsoever in quality, service, speed, availability, responsiveness, convenience, or utility of products and services available in the market (including you and all of your competitors)

- No innovation in the products, services, or systems across the entire market

- No impact from fiscal policies or government regulations and no changes in the economy

In short, the law of demand assumes that the entire world is perfectly static, operating as a commercially sterile laboratory for you to decipher your price elasticity. It assumes that your product or service and everything you wrap around it are perfectly identical to every other company's offer. All of these assumptions are invalid in the real world.

What's the problem with unquestioning belief in the infallibility of this law? Companies undercharge all over the place because of phantom fears of volume loss. It's holding you back from earning higher prices for the excellence of your products and services.

You can test this with marginal price increases in a low-risk area of your business. You'll find that this "law" is more of a loose guideline with a lot of wiggle room than an unerring truth.

How to Make a Data-Driven Decision

If you increase prices, how much volume can you afford to lose and still make the same profit? This is a valuable exercise to undertake.

As we've seen, accurately predicting volume loss is challenging because we notoriously overestimate price sensitivity on the customer's behalf. Knowing exactly where that break-even line is gives you the confidence to pursue a price increase with a realistic understanding of possible outcomes.

In Chapter 16, we'll look at the Price-Volume Trade-Off tool, but here's an example of how it works. The table below shows you the incremental sales volume needed to break even on profit with various price discounts based on your gross margin. Notice the lower-left-hand portion of the table: it is mathematically impossible to grow volume enough to financially offset the cost of the discount!

Volume-Price Break Even Table (Equivalent Profit)

PRICE CHANGE	PRESENT GROSS MARGIN SALES VOLUME CHANGE FOR BREAKEVEN										
	10%	15%	20%	25%	30%	35%	40%	45%	50%	55%	60%
20%	-67%	-57%	-50%	-44%	-40%	-36%	-33%	-31%	-29%	-27%	-25%
15%	-60%	-50%	-43%	-37%	-33%	-30%	-27%	-25%	-23%	-21%	0%
10%	-50%	-40%	-33%	-29%	-25%	-22%	-20%	-18%	-17%	-15%	-14%
5%	-33%	-25%	-20%	-17%	-14%	-11%	-11%	-10%	-9%	-8%	-8%
2%	-17%	-12%	-9%	-7%	-6%	-5%	-5%	-4%	-4%	-4%	-3%
1%	-9%	-6%	-5%	-4%	-3%	-3%	-2%	-2%	-2%	-2%	-2%
-1%	11%	7%	5%	4%	3%	3%	3%	2%	2%	2%	2%
-2%	25%	15%	11%	9%	7%	6%	5%	5%	4%	4%	3%
-5%	100%	50%	33%	25%	20%	17%	14%	12%	11%	10%	9%
-10%		200%	100%	67%	50%	40%	33%	29%	25%	22%	20%
-15%			300%	150%	100%	75%	60%	50%	43%	37%	33%
-20%				400%	200%	133%	100%	80%	67%	57%	50%

Figure 3.4 Sales volume needed to break even
by price change and gross margin

You can see this matches the graphs from Chapter 2 in the section titled "Make It Up in Volume." You may remember the example: A company making 30 percent gross margin requires a 50 percent increase in sales volume *just to break even* with a 10 percent discount. Anything less than 50 percent sales volume growth, and they'll lose money in the bargain.

That company making 30 percent gross margin can afford to lose up to 25 percent of their volume and still make more profit with a 10 percent price increase.

Apex, a company with a 20 percent gross margin, can afford to lose a third of its sales volume with a 10 percent price increase and still break even. The goal, of course, is to lose little to no volume with a variable, risk-mitigated price increase, resulting in a much higher margin. Analysis like this demonstrates that you can withstand some volume loss with a price increase—and your profitability will *improve* even with some volume loss.

Key Takeaways

- Raising prices can lead to increased profitability, even if it results in some loss of sales volume.
- Sales teams often overestimate the negative impact of price increases on sales volume.
- Understanding the break-even point for volume loss post-price increase is crucial for strategic decision-making.
- Losing less profitable customers can sometimes be beneficial.
- Effective pricing strategy involves accepting some customer loss for overall profitability gains.

- Data-driven decision-making in pricing helps overcome fear-based responses to market dynamics.
- Educating sales teams on the complex dynamics of price and volume can improve their confidence.

Client Spotlight: Vern Hydorn, NBM

You might be good at pricing for your business, but are you truly great at it?

Being comfortable with your revenue and margins is not always a good thing for business. Often, it means you have an opportunity to do more.

Take Vern Hydorn, for example. As the head of sales for NBM, a family-owned office products sales and service company, Vern has seen it all. The company has been in business for 40 years, serving 5,000 small- to midsize businesses across multiple industries. Since joining as a recent college graduate in 1987, he's watched NBM grow into a $30 million business, regularly exceeding industry profitability benchmarks. But despite their success, the sales team found themselves in some common traps that prevent companies from achieving true pricing excellence.

"Every metric in our industry we knock out of the park," Hydorn says. "And our margins are strong. We're not afraid to bill for things. We were pretty good at pricing. But that doesn't mean we were *great* at it."

When Hydorn's sales team approached him about pricing for net new customers, his reaction was usually to greenlight what they proposed. "If I'm looking at a new customer and a set of numbers, I'm kind of throwing a dart at a dartboard to say, 'Hey, this is where I think I should be,'" he says. "Well, that comes from my experience, but it's also from my fear of losing in that dartboard throw."

Those self-limiting beliefs—This *is what we can charge*. This *is what the customer will pay. The customer will* never *go for a bigger number*—kept the team from truly understanding their value and pricing accordingly. "You get stuck in these ways of always doing the same thing," Hydorn says. "And you just need someone to kind of tip you over the edge to thinking about something differently."

That tipping point came during training with Boost. The program was pivotal in helping Vern's team step back from fear-driven pricing and instead anchor pricing in the value they were providing. It helped them "get out of their heads," think differently, and price and negotiate with confidence. They embraced a new way of thinking: fear about what the customer will say or that they will walk away is not a reason to be complacent about pricing.

The NBM sales team started to see pricing more and more as a reflection of the value NBM brought to their customers. "Maybe where I think I should be is $25,000. But what if it's $27,000? Now I've got another 10 percent to play with," Hydorn explains. "We just needed to hear that. Take those shackles off, try and throw out that bigger number, and see where you get."

Like his team, Hydorn says that earlier in his career, he was resistant to raising prices out of fear of losing customers. "I don't want to do anything that might alienate a customer, that might get them to think about moving on. It's really, really hard to get a new customer. And so, once you have them, you want to keep them." But he has learned that with all the things you think a customer might say about your prices, "it's almost always worse in your mind than what it turns out to be."

Since the Boost training, Vern has adopted a new approach. When his team presents him with pricing for a new customer, he challenges them to consider if they are fully reflecting the value they're delivering. "The person on the other side of the desk is conditioned to negotiate the best possible situation they can for their organization. So, that friction is already there. If you can just raise the bar, sometimes you'll get it. Sometimes you won't. But if you don't raise the bar, you're *never* going to get it."

Vern's story is a powerful reminder that even when your business is profitable, there is always an opportunity to do better with pricing. Getting stuck in old habits can limit your pricing power.

"We all have these internal battles and conversations, and it's helpful to just free yourself up and say, 'Hey, why not try 5 percent more, or 10 percent more?' Every business could benefit from hearing that message."

PART 2

CUSTOMER TACTICS

It's Human to Try to Save Money

We have to accept an important truth about our customers when we're making decisions about pricing in our organizations: Customers will always want everything cheaper.

As a customer yourself, do you want to save money? Do you want lower prices on the things you buy? Of course you do. It is how we operate as human beings. It's part of our survival instinct—our resources are how we feed and care for ourselves and our families. If your money doubled overnight, would you suddenly be fine parting with a bunch of it or overpaying for things? No! You'd still be concerned with how you spent it. You'd still want to be a smart buyer.

No matter how much we have, we never want to overpay. To hold on to what we have, humans have developed buying strategies and negotiating tactics to save money and even underpay for what we want and need.

Even your best customers—your most loyal customers, value-committed customers who could write a better testimonial about you than you could write about yourself—even those customers are thrilled to underpay you. If you called them and said, "We're cutting our prices by 50 percent," they'd be thrilled.

Everybody is happy to underpay. Because that's how human beings are wired.

You're thinking, *Why is she telling me this? I know how human beings operate. I've been one my whole life. So, what?*

Here's the "so, what." The problem arises when you start to confuse what customers tell you with market intel instead of recognizing it as negotiating tactics.

While customers will always want it cheaper, you don't have to succumb to their tactics to get lower prices. The trick is knowing that this happens, understanding the tactics, and learning how to combat them. In the next three chapters, we'll look at the specific ways your customers try to pay you less than you deserve:

Don't confuse customer negotiation tactics with market intel.

1. They object to your price and compare you to the competition—and you believe that's market intel.
2. They say *yes* to you—and you don't pay attention to it. (Trust me—it happens all the time, as you'll see in Chapter 5!)
3. They tell you your price is too high—and you believe them.

These customer tactics are costing your company money every day. If you charge less than your customers are willing to pay based on the value they derive from your products and services, you are letting them keep *your* money in *their* pockets. In the following chapters, we'll look closely at what customers do to get the lowest possible price.

CHAPTER 4

TACTIC OR MARKET INTEL

Learning Objectives

1. Recognize how customers curate information to influence pricing decisions.
2. Pull back the curtain on the motivation and methods behind customer price objections.
3. Develop approaches to respond effectively to customer pricing tactics.

We work with many clients in the office furniture dealership industry. It's a regional business, and in one city, we worked with the top four office furniture dealers. Together, as competitors, they made up over 80 percent of the market share. These were, indeed, the big dogs.

During separate training programs with their respective sales teams, each firm told my team that they were the highest-priced player in the market. Each one firmly believed they were the most expensive. Can you guess their response when we asked how they knew they were the priciest?

"Our customers told us."

What? Let me get this straight: your certainty of your price position in the market comes to you by way of customers who directly benefit from telling you that?

You cannot believe your customers. Or, put more specifically, you cannot believe your customers about pricing. Even if they are lovely, warm, wonderful, honest people about most things, they are almost never honest about pricing.

Why would they be? It's in their best interest to share only part of the story, to curate information, and to urge you to believe that your prices are (always) higher than everyone else's.

As we say in the pricing biz, buyers are liars.[††]

[††] *Note:* Some of our client sales teams react poorly to the phrase "Buyers are liars." I like it because it's catchy and it rhymes, but I'd encourage you not to get too hung up on the language. If hearing "Buyers are liars" is objectionable to you, reframe it as "Sometimes my customers don't roll out the red carpet of pricing information for me, hoping to get a lower price."

I believe most customers aren't openly lying or maliciously concealing information. Instead, they simply aren't telling the whole truth because they have a job to do, a boss to impress, a business to run, people counting on them. It makes sense that sometimes people aren't completely truthful and transparent, or don't tell the whole story, or maybe even sometimes fib a little bit because they're trying to save a buck. But remember, you have a job to do, too. You have to sell and defend value. Those competing goals create the tension inherent in sales.

During negotiations, customers offer your salespeople information they claim to have about the market—including details about your pricing relative to that of your competitors—and your salespeople naively interpret it as objective data. More alarmingly, they take this as an indication of your customers' willingness to pay you. They mistake your customers' buying strategies and negotiation tactics for market intel.

In other words, your salespeople trust your customers too much. And they do it at their peril because the information customers provide is polluted with their own self-interest. Buyers don't fully and accurately share all the details of their budget, competitive quotes, etc., but that doesn't make them bad people. It is rational for customers to aim for the best products and services at the lowest price.

Remember What It's Like to Be a Buyer When You Sell

Reflect on the last time you made a major purchase, like a car. Consider your interactions with the salesperson, and then answer these questions:

1. Did you embellish some information or withhold some facts from the salesperson?
2. Were you willing to gather information from one salesperson and buy from another?
3. Were you less than 100 percent honest and less than 100 percent transparent with the salespeople you spoke with?

If you answered *yes* to any of these questions, you are perfectly normal. If you answered *no* to every question, you are unusually honest and transparent in your buying habits, even when it costs you money. (Less than 1 percent of our client salespeople have said they never conceal anything during a major purchase. The implication: almost everyone does conceal, curate, or stretch the truth.)

Although you know you aren't always 100 percent honest when you buy, it's easy to forget that other people buy this way when you sell to them. It's all too common to take at face value what customers tell you about pricing, competitive quotes, and their budgets and then respond to that feedback as if it's fact.

Most people engage in these behaviors to get the best deal. Buyers try to secure the best deal, and they don't always tell the whole truth or share transparently and honestly all of the details of their buying process. We know this from being consumers ourselves.

> **Although you know you aren't always 100 percent honest when you buy, it's easy to forget that other people buy this way when you sell to them.**

Do your customers do this to you? Emphatically, yes.

Don't Confuse Buying Tactics with Market Intel

Do not confuse your customer's buying tactics and negotiating strategies with objective data about the value of your products and services. Here are a few truths to consider in the face of this supposed "market intel":

1. **You will only see the quotes where you are the most expensive.** Whether you're dealing with fair, honest people or not, what you're seeing might not be a complete picture of the truth. You walk into a

purchasing meeting, and the buyer has a stack of quotes proving that you're the most expensive. Guess what? The top inch of that stack is where you were the most expensive. The two-inch stack where you were the cheapest is back at the buyer's office, and the other 16 inches of that stack are Grandma's recipes! Customers only tell you when your price is too high.

You won't ever hear when your price is too low. Sometimes, your price is lower than your competitor's price, and you'll never find out how much money you left on the table.

2. **There's no such thing as "the" market price.** No one—not the customer, not the competitor, not you—can pinpoint what "the" market price is because "the" market price doesn't exist. B2B businesses generally have different prices for different customers at different times. Price is a living, breathing, amorphous thing that changes every single time a quote is issued or a deal is closed. So, if you see *one* quote or *one* invoice that is cheaper than yours, it is just *one* data point at *one* moment in time. It is not indicative of market price. (This assumes the quote or invoice is authentic, and sometimes they aren't!) The customer is not operating with perfect information. Neither is your competitor. Nor are you. I believe you and your teams know quite a lot about market pricing, and yet I'm inviting you to consider that your too-fixed idea of "what the market will pay" can result in a self-created price ceiling.

The crucial lesson from this story: Remember that customers are looking for the cheapest price, and they curate the information they give you to get it.

Often, best-in-class providers already earn a price premium, which is great. However, sometimes that leads sellers to think, *We're already the most expensive; we can't charge more.* I promise you, there have been times when you were told you were the most expensive and you weren't. Your team may feel you have nowhere to go with price but down because you're already "the most expensive." I challenge you to explore if that's as true as you think. Furthermore, even if you are earning a premium in the market, are you premium enough? In other words, if you're generating 50 percent better value than your nearest competitor, but your prices are only 30 percent higher, you might be leaving money on the table.

Noisy Data

I'm an engineer and a total geek for data. You may have heard of something called "noisy data": some meaningless piece of information sneaks into your data and corrupts or distorts it, and it affects your decision-making. In sales, this happens when our customers give us information that is misreported, misrepresented, or curated to support their agenda. The problem arises when we believe it. We believe it to be objective data when it's only *noise*.

Our clients frequently say things like, "Our customers tell us our prices are too high," or "They can get the same thing cheaper from a competitor." Or they say, "Our customer has a competitive quote that we need to match," or "There's another provider who can do it for less."

Do these sound familiar to you?

When we hear these things and believe that information, we're in real danger of underpricing. Complaints and price objections are just noise—the only data is sales. They buy, or they don't buy. When the customer buys, you get data that your price is acceptable. When the customer doesn't buy, you get data that your price might be a problem. (It's not the only reason customers don't buy!) When it comes to pricing, sales is data. Complaints are just noise.

Revenue consultant John Harrison says, "You know you're priced right when your customers complain, but buy anyway." Make your decisions from data, not noise.

What Drives the Buy?

I attended a workshop, a few years ago, led by a woman who had been a procurement agent at General Motors. Anyone who knows the automotive industry knows it's one of the most aggressively priced industries there is. She shared that, in 25 years of buying on behalf of GM, she never made a purchasing decision based on price. Not once.

> **When it comes to pricing, sales is data. Complaints are just noise.**

Her number one and number two drivers of her buying decisions were *in stock* and *in spec*. If a part was out of stock or out of spec, it would shut down the line, and if you shut down the line at GM, it would cost tens of thousands of dollars per *minute*. She knew that if *her* choice of a supplier shut down the line, she would be fired. And—no surprise—she was pretty risk-averse on the idea of getting fired.

Now, if she could save the company money with discounts or better pricing, she could get a bonus or a promotion, and those were certainly nice to have. But price was a distant third compared to the issues that could get her fired.

Yet, what did she beat up her vendors about for 25 years? *Price, price, price.* Price did not drive the buy, but it was what she pressed sellers on every time. In the most mercenary and ruthless procurement environment I've ever seen, this buyer admitted to not buying on price.

If customers exaggerate price sensitivity even in the most price-sensitive industry, couldn't it also happen in your industry? Couldn't it also be true of your customers?

An Infamous Procurement Tactic

Have you ever been told this by a procurement professional?

We've prequalified several vendors who can supply our needs with the quality, speed, availability, service, and specifications we require. Congratulations on being one of those vendors! Now, please submit your bid, and we will choose from among those prequalified vendors based on who has the lowest price. Since you're all pre-qualified according to the same criteria, the only factor at this point is price.

Ay, ay, ay—that old chestnut! Then, if you have the (mis)fortune to win, they often come back to you again and ask you to submit your best and final price. The gall.

Here's the thing: They. Are. Lying. (At least, sometimes.) I have seen behind the curtain. I've sat in meeting rooms and offices of corporate America with procurement agents who have admitted that they prefer Vendor XYZ over Vendor ABC because they are substantially more responsive, even though the product quality and manufacturing tolerances are pretty much identical. They've further admitted to a willingness to choose Vendor XYZ for that reason, even if they weren't the cheapest bid. I've witnessed this multiple times.

Don't believe me? This was the exact situation admitted to by the GM procurement officer in this chapter.

An important lesson from the GM story in the sidebar is the need to discover what really drives the buying decision. What are the customer's priorities *besides price*? What do they value, and what do they value most?

Instead of accepting what your customers and prospects say about your pricing, their budget, and your competition at face value, there are a few things your salespeople can do to break the cycle:

1. **Think differently.** You need to think differently before you can act differently. Remember that you may not be getting the truth, or at least not the entire truth. It's important to go into pricing discussions with a healthy dose of skepticism. Your customers are going to tell you what they need to tell you in order to get the price they want, and that is always going to be carefully curated information. Knowing this will help your salespeople hold their ground on price when faced with pushback.

2. **Prepare.** Figuring out ahead of time how to diplomatically push back on price objections or ask for more information is important to preserving the relationship. Brainstorm what kind of price pushback you're likely to hear so you can be ready with questions to probe deeper. Incorporate learning from prior customer conversations. When did you take something that a customer told you at face value? What could you have asked at that moment?

3. **Practice.** Before you're with your customer, practice out loud what you will say when faced with price objections and "market intel." Role-play with colleagues and managers, or even in front of a mirror,

until it becomes second nature to request more information.

If you believe what your customer tells you about how much they will pay for your goods and services, you've already lost the pricing excellence game. Instead, apply a healthy dose of skepticism and ask more questions when your customers share pricing information.

> **If you believe what your customer tells you about how much they will pay for your goods and services, you've already lost the pricing excellence game.**

Customers will always ask for better pricing. That is evidence of only one thing: their human instinct to hold onto resources at work. They're protecting something, be it their job, bonus, company's profits, or employees. Your faulty conclusion that your products and services are somehow overpriced because of this "intel" is causing you to underprice and costing you substantial margin.

Key Takeaways

- Information provided by customers during negotiations often reflects their self-interest rather than objective market data.
- Sales teams need to develop healthy skepticism toward customer-provided price comparisons.
- Understanding the underlying reasons behind customer price complaints is crucial for effective pricing negotiations.

- Recognizing different customer buying tactics can help sales teams respond more effectively.
- Sales conversations should focus on uncovering the real value drivers for customers beyond price.
- Developing skills to probe deeper into customer motivations can reveal true buying criteria, which is the key to unlocking pricing power.

Client Spotlight: Peter Argondizzo, Argo Translation

For Argo Translation, a translation services firm founded in 1995, increasing prices required three things: confidence, data, and candid conversations with clients.

"We had some folks here who really bought into 'the lever I have [to close deals] is pricing,' like, 'This client is pushing back, let me drop the price,'" says Peter Argondizzo, Argo's founder and president. "And I think that came from a lack of confidence in the product or the service. That's where we struggled a little, and some of those people aren't here anymore. It took that level of commitment to the message, and it also took [looking into] the inner workings" of the company, like how they priced for different clients and different levels of service.

Building that confidence required training salespeople and project managers to understand the value of what they provide and to convey that consistently to their clients. "It's really about confidence and understanding your own services and products well enough to communicate to clients what they're getting," Argondizzo says.

Once salespeople understood the impact of even a small discount, they were able to focus more on tailoring services to fit the client's needs; they were able to differentiate between the client who needs "A+++ service" and the client who needs less. "You can do pricing concessions," Argondizzo says, "but then you have to take something away."

Confidence also came into play when dealing with "third-quote" customers: those customers who needed to satisfy a procurement process requiring three quotes, even when they had no intention of considering switching to Argo. Argondizzo says they had to be comfortable with losing customers who didn't engage or don't want to talk about what's important to them; they just wanted the right number. "We have very little customer attrition, but we've lost a couple of those types of customers... The conversation has to be that we don't really want to be your third quote anymore."

Having confidence was just one piece of the puzzle when it came to raising prices. They also turned to data to discover what their clients prioritized and where salespeople were conceding on price unnecessarily.

They now have monthly pricing meetings where they look at scattergram data (see Chapter 15) for all clients, as well as at a dashboard where they can see the profit margin based on each project manager by customer. With the dashboard, "We can very quickly understand: Is there a problem? Where? Is it this customer? Is that project manager giving stuff away? We can quickly drill down and see that at our fingertips, which we never had or realized how important that data was."

The data showed they were conceding on price too readily, they weren't charging for certain work they were paying their employees to do, and customers weren't as price-sensitive as they thought they were. "What we discovered was that a huge percentage of our clients wanted customer service, they wanted to be handled appropriately, they wanted the extra attention—and the benefits that extra attention provides. And we realized that they weren't really price-sensitive. This was negative self-talk. So, we finally were able to charge what we would consider a market price... Now, [because of higher prices that reflected our value], we had a little bit of rocket fuel; suddenly, we have funds to invest in better technology and better people. And suddenly, we're even providing better service to the client."

The third step was having candid, and sometimes difficult, conversations with clients about price. Salespeople learned that they had to talk with customers about what was important to them as well as help them understand why the company was charging a price premium for their work. That meant talking to the customer about the cost of failure.

Now, his salespeople say, "We can lower the cost. But here are the things that are going to suffer when we lower the cost. Or we can do it faster. But here are the parts we must skip to do it fast," Argondizzo says.

Even though these conversations can be difficult for both the salesperson and the client, if they don't have that dialogue, "we're not able to rightsize the service to where they need it to be," he says. By talking honestly with their clients about what goes into each project and taking into account their needs, Argo's salespeople find that clients are better able to see the value the company provides: they'll decide that they can accept a standard timeline because "it's going to be less expensive, and it's going to be higher quality. Why wouldn't you want it?"

"In our industry, you probably have two [types of providers]—the ones that pull the price lever, they just raise prices with no added value, and those that have to sell an amazing volume to keep the doors open because they operate at such a low margin. I think neither one is good," Argondizzo says. By building confidence, applying data, and having candid conversations internally and with clients, they were able to raise prices and maintain their strong client relationships and high levels of customer service.

Commanding higher prices has generated substantial profitability that Argondizzo poured back into the business to make it stronger. "Our client relationships have gotten tighter, and we're providing a higher level of service because now we're very focused" when it comes to pricing. "We've added staff, we've been able to add bandwidth, and I think our clients appreciate it."

CHAPTER 5

WHAT DOES "YES" MEAN?

Learning Objectives

1. Understand the concept of an "automatic *yes*" and its implications on customer perceptions.
2. Utilize *auto-yeses* to build team confidence and identify business opportunities.
3. Grasp the opportunity presented by hearing *no* and losing deals.

When sales teams tell me that all they hear from customers is that their prices are too high, I ask, "Have you *ever* quoted a product or service at a price to a customer who replied *yes?* In other words, you proposed a price, and they accepted the price you offered without objection. If this has happened to you, you have received what I call an *auto-yes*—an automatic *yes*."

If you've ever told a customer your price and they accepted that price without a negotiation, you have received an auto-yes.

An *auto-yes* is data from your customers that your pricing is fair, competitive, realistic, on point, or possibly too low.

You *do* get data from your customers that your pricing is fair or too low. You just don't pay attention to it. You win that business, hand off the order to operations, and go right back to selling to the complainers who tell you that your prices are too high.

What is at work here is *negativity bias*, a concept from

> An auto-yes is data from your customers that your pricing is fair, competitive, realistic, on point, or, possibly, too low.

psychology where humans recall negative events with greater frequency and intensity than positive events. We had to hear 20 compliments to make up for one incident with the schoolyard bully when we were a child. This bias shows up in our sales life too. You can win 20 deals and then, lose one and think, "Oh no, our prices are too high!"

How this relates to *auto-yeses* is that you don't pay attention to the times customers buy from you at the price you quoted. However infrequently this happens, this is data from customers that your prices are fair or too low. Don't let it sail without noticing! You pay a lot of attention to the price objections and the lost deals, concluding that "all your customers" tell you that your prices are too high.

It's time to pay attention to the auto-yeses because they benefit you in two crucial ways: they boost your confidence, and they give you useful data.

Mine Auto-Yeses for Confidence and Data

The first thing to mine from *auto-yeses* is confidence. In not so many words, the customer is complimenting you on your value, letting you know the price is more than fair. Grab ahold of that confidence. Remember: we discount from a fear of phantom volume loss. The antidote to that fear is confidence, and we have to get it anywhere we can because customers don't love to hand it to us.

> A *yes* feels great, but you need to hear *no* sometimes, or you won't know if you're bumping up against the market price.

The second thing you can mine from auto-yeses is data about where you might have underpriced opportunities in your business.

Let's return to the question I asked at the beginning of the chapter: Do you ever give a price to a customer, and they say *yes* without negotiation? As a pricing consultant, if I hear you say, "Yes, 100 percent of the time; we never lose to competitors, and customers never argue about pricing," I'll tell you that winning all the deals is a red flag. A *yes* feels great, but you need to hear *no* sometimes, or you won't know if you're bumping up against the market price.

Now, you may say, "Don't worry—we hear *no*. We have competitors; we lose business; we have to negotiate. We don't have a 100 percent auto-yes rate!" To that, I ask whether your auto-yes rate is "too high" for some types of customers or products or services or opportunities. Do you rarely get pushback under certain circumstances, such as when the customer is in a huge rush? In other words, when you start to dissect your business and data, if you have a very high auto-yes rate in some chunks of your business, it's an opportunity.

Akin to auto-yes is win rate. Is there any part of your business where your win rate is high, possibly even too high? Maybe it's happening with certain kinds of customers, products, services, geographic segments, or under certain circumstances. "Yeah, you know what, our European OEM customers buy this brand of flanges... we really never hear any complaints about the price." Or "Money is no object when someone needs a rush on a tax audit project."

Do you have any segments of your business with a high auto-yes rate or too high a win rate? If so, there may be an opportunity for you to raise prices in those areas.

The Surprising Opportunity of Losing Over Price

I just told you that you sometimes need to lose over price. It's no fun, but it's necessary. When it happens, what do you do? Generally, salespeople drop their chin, kick the dirt, and lose more pricing confidence.

Most sellers fail to capitalize on the brilliant opportunity that such a moment presents.

A client who sells professional services told me that they've been facing more competitive pressure. When I asked if they'd seen a drop in their win rate, they didn't

> Customers indicate price as the reason for choosing a competitor because it's the easy way out.

know. (Are they paying more attention to the *no*, or are they truly hearing *no* more? Is negativity bias at work?)

If they are hearing *no* more, what's really going on?

Customers indicate price as the reason for choosing a competitor because it's the easy way out. It's more expedient and polite than telling you that you didn't make a compelling case for your value proposition. "Your price is too high" often means "Your price is too high for the value you provide."

Or, more accurately, "Your price is too high for the value I *perceive* that you provide."

When you hear, "We went with your competitor because of price," it's worth digging a little deeper. Ask questions to uncover what's really going on:

- Was there a different problem that you didn't solve for them?
- Did you leave boxes unchecked?
- Did you connect your solution to their key pain points?
- Did they perceive value in what your product or service provides?

One question I love to recommend for opening this conversation is, "If we could have erased the difference in price between our proposal and our competitor's, who would you have chosen?"

If the customer still would have chosen your competitor, price was never the problem. You have more digging to do.

If the customer would have chosen you at equalized pricing, ask why. Some questions to consider:

- What about our proposal would have made you choose *us* if the prices had been the same?
- What about our proposed solution was a great fit for you?
- Besides price, what concerns did you have about our proposal? Did we miss the mark somewhere else?

- What could have been different about our proposal that would have led you to choose us at our proposed price?
- Under what circumstances would you have chosen our proposal?

Don't rubber-stamp "price" as the reason for losses. Mine those losses for additional insights about gaps in your offering or your ability to communicate its value.

Key Takeaways

- Frequent *auto-yeses* can be a sign of underpricing and missed revenue opportunities.
- Negativity bias can lead sales teams to overemphasize price objections, overlooking positive pricing feedback.
- *Auto-yeses* are an untapped source of market data, revealing customer satisfaction with pricing.
- Using *auto-yes* feedback can strengthen sales confidence and reduce fear-based discounting.

Client Spotlight: Steve Voelzke, Robroy Industries, Electrical Products Division

Relentless focus on value is a key to higher prices for Robroy Industries' Electrical Products Division, a fourth-generation family-owned manufacturer of niche electrical products led by President Steve Voelzke.

Because Robroy sells into a complex value chain of stakeholders—end users, engineering firms, contractors, distributors, and independent sales reps, creating pull-through demand with a rock-solid value proposition is critical to reducing system-wide price sensitivity.

To earn higher prices in traditionally price-sensitive channels such as distribution, Robroy focused on demand creation through education and direct engagement with end users and specifiers, ensuring that the value proposition was clear and compelling before pricing discussions even began. This proactive stance meant that when it came time to negotiate prices, the groundwork was already laid, when "it really becomes more of a formality," Voelzke says.

Robroy's team focuses on creating and maintaining a value proposition that justifies their pricing. "At the end of the day, you spend more money to make a niche product. We add a lot more value to that niche product than our competitors do. And for that reason, we can command a higher price... We can charge more because the customer is getting more value. They're getting their job accomplished. They can rest easy that they don't have to worry," Voelzke said. The team has greater confidence when facing price objections, knowing the extensive work and value proposition backing their prices.

Working with Boost helped Voelzke's team see that they were on the right path. "We've been on this path for a while, and I think we really do a decent job overall. But Casey gave us some more formality around it that we'll continue to build into our systems," Voelzke said.

Concepts like the cost of failure became integral to their sales pitch, emphasizing the risks their products mitigated. Voelzke shared, "Cost of failure is huge for us. We've already played with that quite a bit: what are the risks [of using a cheaper alternative]?"

Voelzke shared the power of another concept learned in the Boost training, give-to-get. "Where there's a need to negotiate on price, we can maybe get something else, like a bigger part of the project or another project where we're not specified or where maybe the value proposition isn't understood as clearly. That's another thing that our team has done much better since the training."

Additionally, the idea of "hot sauce" items—small but crucial components that drive overall system sales—was leveraged to enhance their product offering and pull through more sales.

Robroy's investment in a pricing training program has paid for itself multiple times over, but Voelzke recognizes the need to plan for more training to maintain clarity and confidence: "We'll maintain the engagement because you have [new] people that come in… just to maintain that consistency. That's the whole thing: you do it once well, but you need to keep on top of it. You'll learn something new every time you go through it."

CHAPTER 6

"YOUR PRICE IS TOO HIGH"

Learning Objectives

1. Explore the real reasons behind customers' claims that prices are too high.
2. Learn to distinguish between genuine price concerns and negotiation tactics.
3. Develop skills to effectively respond when customers challenge pricing.

In Chapter 5, we saw that auto-yeses are a signal of unexercised pricing power in the nooks and crannies of your business. Auto-yeses can also give your sales team a much-needed confidence boost when they're feeling beat up on price from every side.

But getting beat up on price is a signal too—one that can be incredibly valuable for your salespeople when you're making decisions about pricing for your business.

While hearing objections to your price feels awful, I'd like you to consider that price objections and even losing business over price are important parts of a good pricing strategy.

I'm going to say that again because it can be counter-intuitive: A strong and effective pricing strategy requires you to lose business sometimes and to hear price pushback. If you aren't losing business from time to time over price, then your prices are too low.

This probably feels paradoxical, but it's true nonetheless. When customers give your salespeople price pressure or push them for a better number, they're actually giving them a buying signal: the customer wants to buy from you.

All of your customers— whether you sell in a B2B,

> If you aren't losing business from time to time over price, then your prices are too low.

B2C, B2G, or nonprofit environment; whether you sell a product or a service; whether your solution sells for $1 or $1 billion—are human beings. And like all human beings, they're deeply self-interested. They don't want to waste their time. Why would they bother telling your salespeople to sharpen their pencils or match your competitor's price or any other thing they say to get the product or service for less if they had no interest in buying from them? The answer is they wouldn't. They'd just go buy from someone else.

Customers push salespeople for better pricing; they give them last look; they ask them to match the competitor's price because they have at least *some* interest in buying from them. And that means salespeople have *some* pricing power over their customers. Your sales team must use that power as a permission slip. They must use it to crack open the sales conversation and ask questions to find out why the customer is putting price pressure on them in the first place. Your salespeople may find out something that indicates there's no need to discount after all. Or they may find a deeper buying need, a customer issue they can address that makes something besides price the primary concern.

Even if the seller asks questions and concludes they still need to discount, nothing was lost by asking questions. At the end of this questioning process, sellers can still use discounting as a sales tactic—it just shouldn't be the first tactic they reach for. Remember: although it's unpleasant, price pressure has an upside. The customer is saying, "I'm interested in buying *your* products or services."

Let's break the customers who say, "Your price is too high" into four groups because, while their message is the same, their underlying price sensitivity is not. In other words, their actual walk-away point, the point at which they will not buy from you, is different. Let's explore how to identify these customers and the effective strategies your sales team can use when working with them.

1. Professional Buyers and Constitutional Hagglers

The first group of people includes purchasing agents and professional buyers—people who beat you up on price for a living. I'm going to add to this group the people who beat you up on price for fun and sport. (My brother is in this category. He's the cheapest person I know on the planet.)

For the people in this category, no price is low enough that they won't argue. These people have never given an *auto-yes* in their life. That's just not how they operate.

You could be negotiating a deal with a purchasing agent or someone like my cheapo brother: "We're running an amazing sale today. One day only. You have to cut us a PO today, but if you do, we will do this $42,000 worth of work for you for $1." My brother would say, "I don't know—seems kind of pricey. How about fifty cents?" Purchasing agents are given bonuses and promoted based on their ability to do this to your salespeople. They will negotiate, guaranteed.

Some salespeople operate in industries where they cannot avoid selling to people like this daily. Whether you sell to trained buyers and procurement professionals or not, every seller runs into this type of negotiator eventually. Is it reasonable or rational to let these people inform your sales team's confidence about their pricing? It is not. The customer's need to fight aggressively over price is not data nor market intel. It is an aggressive game that some people play for a living. Some people play it for fun. But if your salespeople are selling to a buyer like this, what does the buyer's price objection say about the value of your products or services?

Nothing.

But that won't stop your salespeople from feeling *beat up* about it. They walk out of those aggressive negotiations, tails between their legs, carrying that loss of confidence right into the next deal. They're so stung that they underprice that next deal or are quicker to offer a discount.

The problem is that salespeople respond to these buyer tactics as if those tactics are market intel. They are not. They are tactics. Remember: no number the seller could have proposed would be low enough to prevent the buyer from employing the same tactic.

My advice to salespeople for dealing with these customers is to reset after one of those negotiations. Reset, reset,

reset. It's a game they are playing. Be prepared, play the game, do your best, take your licks, and reset. You'll find no data in that negotiation. Make your peace with whatever happens and release the belief that any information you hear from the customer is market intel. Comfort yourself, knowing that there is not a single number you could say to that person that wouldn't result in the same tactic.

2. "Can't Hurt to Ask" Club

We talked about this next category of customers in Chapter 2—the "Can't Hurt to Ask" Club. (I'd wager we're all members of this club.)

In the negotiation scenario in Chapter 2, I talked about the customer who, when your salesperson tells them the price is $42,000, says, "I'd really love to work with you, but I have several other quotes significantly lower. You don't have to be the lowest, but you have to be close. Is there any way you could do this for $39,000?"

Meanwhile, you may remember that the buyer had a maximum price of $45,000 in mind going into that negotiation.

Now, whatever happens next—whether your salesperson does a beautiful job of value selling the customer on $42,000 or discounts to $39,000, or they meet somewhere in the middle—is irrelevant. Irrelevant. Your salesperson likely walks out of that meeting thinking, *She said she got several other quotes. Good to know the kinds of prices our competitors are quoting...* In other words, your salesperson concludes information about market pricing from the conversation, but that was just a tactic, not market intel. Do you know what market intel your seller never got from the customer?

That she was willing to pay your salesperson as much as $45,000, but he never got that number from her.

It's easy to conclude the wrong information from our customer interactions. Your salesperson can safely conclude one thing from their customer interactions about price — that the customer is doing what human beings do: trying to hold on to their pile of gold.

No matter whether the customer is a business, a consumer, government agency, or a nonprofit, they want to hold on to their piles of gold. My advice to salespeople: Don't conclude your price is too high because the customer engages in ubiquitous tactics to get lower prices.

3. Price Match Requesters

When sales teams tell me they hold limited pricing power because of competition, they often cite competitive price match requests as a prime example. Do you ever get compared to competitive quotes—so-called "last looks"—and asked to match their quote? Let's unpack this tactic used by the third group.

The customer says, "Competitor XYZ can do the same thing for 5 percent less. If you'll match their price, I'll buy from you."

The message beneath the words is, "Competitor XYZ is inferior to you in a way I'm not going to disclose, and I hope you don't figure it out. I'm trying to trick you into giving away your superior quality and service and excellence for their low price. Will you fall for it?"

Let's be clear: If Competitor XYZ were cheaper and better, the customer would buy from Competitor XYZ. They wouldn't bother asking you to match the price. You wouldn't be on the phone, exchanging emails, or standing in their office. The entire conversation only occurs for one reason: the competitor is cheaper, but *you are better*. This customer is simply using the price match request tactic to get your stuff for less.

Your salespeople must see a price match request for what it is: an objective statement of preference for your product, service, and company. The customer doesn't want Competitor XYZ; they want you. I'll go further: a price match request is a love letter from your customer. They don't love Competitor XYZ; they love you. Yes, that's right: they love you.

Now, this is not a moment for arrogance, rather, a moment for questions. Why? Because your salesperson doesn't know why the customer "loves you" or by how much. They have to figure that out. If they love your offering a lot, the price match request is just a tactic, and you've no need to match the price. If they only love your offering a little, your salesperson may decide to price match, or, at least, make some price concession.

> Your salespeople must see a price match request for what it is: an objective statement of preference for your product, service, and company.

Five Costly Seller Mistakes When Asked to Price Match

1. **Match the competitor's price.** I don't love this tactic because it costs you money. And it's often completely avoidable.

2. **Meet in the middle.** Again, this costs money. And even though it's less costly than dropping down to the competitor's price, this meet-in-the-middle

strategy still leaks valuable profit dollars when the customer is often willing to pay our full price.

3. **Employ the "fruit salad" approach.** The customer says so-and-so can do it for less, and then the sales team rushes in to see if the quotes are apples-to-apples. They compare their quote, line by line, with the competitor's, trying to make sure the customer understands why they're better. One problem with the fruit salad approach is that it presumes the customer cares about everything being compared, and they don't. In addition, it often leads to mistake 4, descoping.

4. **Reduce the scope of the proposal.** This is, often, a direct result of apples-to-apples comparison. And it costs you money because you have removed revenue-producing features, products, or services.

5. **Vomit value messaging at the customer.** I don't love this tactic either because—guess what?—they just told you they love you more! You'll never figure out why or how much if you do all the talking. You are busy giving a monologue, telling them how great you are when what you should be doing is having a dialogue. What do they value about your products/services/team? Why do they keep coming back to you? If your ears are closed and your mouth is open, it should be the other way around.

I'm not saying never dive into proposal details to make sure quotes are apples-to-apples. I'm not saying never reduce scope. I'm not even saying never discount. But definitely don't do any of those things first. You can always employ those tactics later but don't start there. Start with questions to figure out how much the customer prefers you over your competition.

Many ways uncover what's important to the customer and what they value in your proposal (signaling why they love you and how much), but here's a simple example: Ask, "Let's imagine for a second that we could wave a wand over these deals and erase the price difference. You'd go with our proposal?" (Yes.) "Okay, so that I can come back to you with a revised proposal that reflects everything that's important to you, can you tell me what it is about our proposal/product/service/team that has you say you'd choose us?" Then, shut up and listen. (See the sidebar "WAIT." Don't fill the silence. Listen!) What will come out of that conversation may tell you how much pricing power you have in that situation.

Salespeople must do this artfully and diplomatically because customers don't love to hand over pricing power. They're no dummies; they won't candidly reveal why you're a better choice for them—they know that hurts their negotiating position. But if sellers engage the customer in a dialogue about what's important to them, some crucial information may be revealed: maybe XYZ can't do it in time, or the product gives them higher shrinkage in the manufacturing process. If your salespeople find that the customer's preference for you is strong, you have pricing power and you don't need to price match.

A second possible outcome of this dialogue is that you won't learn anything about why they love you or how much because they stonewall you to avoid giving up any pricing power. What I tell sellers in this situation is: You are in the same spot you were in before you tried to uncover why they love you—not worse! It costs you nothing but a couple of minutes, and now you still have the option of apples-to-apples, descoping, or offering a discount.

Or maybe, as a third possibility, your salespeople find that the level of preference for you over your competition is low. The customer convinces your salesperson that they don't prefer your products and services enough for them to be worth much of a premium at all. The salesperson may decide to price match or try to get the customer to meet in the middle. Sometimes, this is commercially and competitively the right thing to do. If they decide to price match—if that is the right thing to do—they can't let it cut their confidence. The customer still wants them more, as evidenced by the price match request itself, so they should let that knowledge lift their confidence.

I've seen salespeople walking around all beat up, saying things like, "Viking is kicking our butt—six times, in the last month alone, some-body's price matched us against Viking." Really? Six times in the last month alone somebody loved you more than Viking? Put those love letters on the wall. Reframe how you think about the price match request. It is a compliment from the customer. Take it as the compliment it is.

> **A price match request is a compliment from the customer.**

WAIT

In this chapter, I've shared my dislike for salespeople vomiting value messages at the customer. I think this happens because salespeople are, by and large, uncomfortable with price negotiations and they get nervous.

When salespeople get nervous, they develop a motor-mouth problem. They fill *all* the silence. They talk too much, and they shoot themselves in the foot when it comes to their pricing power. One thing I recommend is for people in pricing negotiations to slow down, pause, and remember this acronym: WAIT.

It stands for **Why Am I Talking?** Why am I talking?

It's important to not fill the silence with too much talking because we may offer something up that we shouldn't and miss an opportunity to listen to the customer and learn what they really care about and what they think of our pricing.

Sometimes a salesperson communicates a price to a customer, and the customer responds with silence. (This is a negotiation tactic commonly taught to procurement professionals, by the way.)

Then, the salesperson gets in their own head. They start making assumptions about what the customer is thinking. They worry that the customer thinks the price is too high and will say *no*. They rush in and fill the silence with price concessions.

So, if you have a tendency to ramble on when you get nervous, remember: WAIT—Why am I talking?

4. Prospects

Prospects are the fourth group we'll talk about. Those possible clients are nearly always going to be more price-sensitive than the customers who love you. Your existing customers know you're worth it. A happy customer who is satisfied by your excellent products and services is, generally, less price-sensitive than someone who doesn't know you. Prospects don't trust your promises yet. They don't know that your quality, reliability, and service are top-notch.

When it comes to prospects, their doubt in your promises masquerades as price sensitivity. What does that mean? I can best illustrate this with an example from my own business:

Our team delivers pricing training programs that help companies increase pricing and profits. Let's imagine a CEO of a $100 million annual revenue company asks us for a proposal for a pricing training program for his sales team. So, I give him the proposal, and I share with him that, conservatively, he can expect a 1 percent lift in price from our work together, given the nature of his industry, value proposition, sales team, and competition.

When he sees the proposal, he tells me the program is too expensive.

Now, 1 percent of $100 million is a million bucks. Our program doesn't cost anywhere near a million bucks. Any rational CEO would trade the much smaller check for our program for the larger return of a million dollars of price lift. So, I don't think he's saying the program is too expensive. I think he's saying, "It's too expensive *if I don't get my million dollars of price lift.*"

I give him our guarantee: If you aren't satisfied qualitatively or quantitatively with the results of our work together, now or ever, we'll refund your money. If you don't get the financial benefits you expect or the behavior change you expect in your people, we'll refund your money. I also tell him we've **never had a customer ask for their money back.** When I make this guarantee, I communicate my complete confidence that we can deliver on our end of the bargain. The customer's risk goes down, and what goes down with it? Their price sensitivity! Why? Because it was never about the price in the first place!

Sometimes, a customer's price objection isn't a price objection at all. It's doubt about your value prop *masquerading* as a price objection! They say, "Your price is too high" or "This is too expensive" or "It costs too much" (which sure feel like price objections!), but I invite you to consider the second part of the sentence they aren't saying:

- Your price is too high *if you don't deliver on time.*
- This is too expensive *if the quality isn't there.*
- It costs too much *if you don't deliver on my creative vision.*
- Your price is too high *if you don't solve my problem.*
- This is too expensive *if you don't meet spec.*
- It costs too much *if you aren't better than the other guy in the ways you claim.*

In other words, the price isn't the problem. The true problem is that they're worried about *what they'll get* for the price.

So, I invite you to consider that, some of the time, when customers say you're too expensive, what they really mean is: I don't trust you. *Yet.*

> **The price isn't the problem. The true problem is that they're worried about *what they'll get* for the price.**

And anything you can do to reduce that risk for them will take away price sensitivity and build their trust.

Consider this: Every one of your competitors is making the same promises as you.

Everyone says they deliver the best products and services with the best customer service, *blah, blah, blah*. The customer sees these claims and may have difficulty making an objective comparison. Often, the only objective information they have for comparison between competitors is pricing. The more confidence your salespeople can give the customer that your product or service *truly* is better, the less focused they'll be on pricing.

How can your salespeople do this? Some companies use guarantees and warranties, as we do, but you don't have to do that. It's not appropriate for every business model nor for every hidden customer concern. You can handle this in many different ways, and it depends on what the customers' fear is about. If they're afraid about you being late, show them your on-time, in-full shipment report, which demonstrates your consistently high results. If they're worried about the quality, give them a free sample. Take the prospect to lunch with an existing customer who can talk about your superb quality. Give them a tour of your facility and show them your airtight processes for exceptional service. The easiest and most effective way? Spend more time and build more trust.

Do whatever it takes to build their confidence that your products and services are just as good as you say. Because until your customers have reason to trust your promises, they will focus on price. And you don't want that.

Lowering the price doesn't solve the customer's core concern, *and* it costs you enormous profit. Invest in reducing your customers' doubt in your promises, and their price sensitivity will drop too.

> **Until your customers have reason to trust your promises, they will focus on price.**

Sell from Confidence

"Your price is too high" is rarely just about price. Your customer may be incentivized to get a lower price from you, or they're testing the waters. Perhaps they're not yet convinced that you will deliver on your promises. Your sales team must remember that buying strategies and negotiating tactics are not market intel. They prove only that your customer is being a human—trying to hold on to their money.

When you sell like the customer has all the power, you sell from fear and discount unnecessarily. The customer needs and benefits from what you sell. Why not your products? Why not your services? So, sell from confidence. Get paid what you're worth.

Key Takeaways

- Price objections often signal customer interest rather than outright rejection.
- Not all "your price is too high" statements reflect true price sensitivity; some are negotiation tactics.
- Losing some business over price can be part of an effective pricing strategy.
- Different types of price-objecting customers require tailored reactions.
- Price-match requests often imply customer preference for your product or service.
- Handling price objections requires a mix of tactical responses and value reinforcement.
- Helping your team understand the nuances of price objections can improve their pricing discussions and the perceived value of the offering.

Client Spotlight:
Joe Parker, Automated Logistics Systems

Losing a client never feels good. But, sometimes, it gives you the push you need to reshape your pricing strategy and culture.

Joe Parker, president of ALS, a logistics and supply chain company providing freight-management services, recalls how losing a major customer over pricing forced his company to face shrinking profit margins in an increasingly competitive market.

"Our largest customer put all their freight out to bid, and we were not prepared for it," Parker says. "Next thing you know, we were $2 million too high, and there was no way we could match. And so, we thought, from then on, that the larger the customer, the more margin you have to give up."

This mindset—that customers controlled pricing—became ingrained. ALS attacked the problem of shrinking profits by hiring more people, thinking it would make them more efficient. But as labor costs rose, they continued to have lower margins. Still, they feared that raising prices would lead to losing customers.

In the sales team's first session with Boost, they confronted this lack of pricing confidence head-on. The message of that session, Parker recalls, was clear: "Profit is not bad. You are in business to make money. If you don't make money, you're not in business."

Over the course of the training, the sales team moved from thinking customers controlled pricing to realizing they had the power to set and control their own prices. This transformational shift led them to create a number of "pricing rituals."

One ritual was the "Corner Club." In this weekly meeting, salespeople identified low-margin customers and used situational awareness—understanding the customer's situation with regard to price sensitivity—to justify rate increases. They ensured that services were priced according to their true value and that no high-quality service was given away for free.

Belief in situational pricing gave ALS the agility to adapt rates based on market conditions and customer needs. They communicated transparently with customers about the broader market environment, reinforcing their partnership and maintaining business relationships amid changes.

An unexpected benefit of this practice was that it led to a higher standard of service at ALS. The team took pride in delivering exceptional value, ensuring that customers who paid higher prices received impeccable service. Customers, Parker says, "ended up getting more value out of our price increase."

In other words, redefining their pricing structure and approach was a win-win.

"When you talk about saving the company," Parker says, "that's literally what [Casey] did." Margins improved by 2 percent within the first year, translating to a $2 million boost in revenue and bottom-line profit. "It's been really transformational in our company, understanding the positive impact of being in charge of your pricing."

PART 3

PRICING OPPORTUNITIES

Where Is Price Sensitivity Already Low?

We've explored how customers use predictable tactics to get your products and services for less. It often feels like every customer is price-sensitive on everything. But there are pockets of unexercised pricing power in your business where customer price sensitivity is low, or at least lower.

Most businesses have unexercised pricing power in two areas:

1. **Where customers aren't paying as much attention.** These could be products, services, or fees that are not as important to them. In these places, price

sensitivity is already low because their pricing focus is elsewhere.

2. **Where you're underpriced relative to your value.** You're the Lexus of your industry being compared to the Corolla. But you're not extracting the premium price for your premium value.

We can't use a butter knife to evenly spread our pricing policy on every deal. We have to be surgical and strategic in our approach. We have to use a scalpel. And we have to apply it where we have *unexercised pricing power*.

In the next two chapters, we'll focus on what we can do to counteract customer tactics when price sensitivity is already low. And then, in Part 4, we'll look at how to sell value to close the gap from underpricing relative to value.

What Is Price Sensitivity and Context?

Price sensitivity is the degree to which price drives demand. It is not constant by customer or product or service. It is *context specific*. A classic example is movie theater popcorn. We'll spend $8 on a tub of popcorn at the movie theater that would cost us $0.25 to make at home.

Here's an example from my personal life. My first child was born in the middle of a record heatwave in 2007. It had been close to 100 degrees outside for about ten days in a row. I had a four-day-old baby at home. So, it was 100 degrees outside and 68 degrees inside. Everything was cool. Until the air conditioner stopped working. A side note: having grown up in a blue-collar home, I'll typically call around and get several quotes if something breaks in my home. I will read those quotes in detail to ensure I'm making a prudent decision.

But on the day of the great air conditioning crisis of 2007, I was focused on *Who can come right now and get this air conditioner fixed? Here's my checkbook. Here's my credit card. Just get this thing fixed.* That day, I had no price sensitivity whatsoever.

Your customers, in the same way, are context-specific in their price sensitivity. And context doesn't just mean "in a hurry." I paid a premium for faster service when my air conditioner went out, but the same thing happens when your customer is coming off a bad experience with one of your competitors, they need extra service or support, their standards are higher, or their risk tolerance is lower. You may pay your accountant $X typically, but when the IRS is auditing you, are you willing to pay more?

When have you been willing to spend a premium for something under certain conditions?

Of course, the magnitude of the price tag you attach to that context specificity must fit inside a morally and commercially appropriate box. You see this going wrong for Pharma Bro, or in the EpiPen story, or for people who try to charge $70 for a case of water after a natural disaster, right? But I don't worry about that for you.

Actually, I worry about the opposite. I worry that you're so morally and commercially appropriate—you're so worried about being good partners to your customers and not gouging them—that you don't charge for things you could. What I know, having done this for hundreds of companies who take extraordinary care of their customers, is that most great companies do many things for free. This is probably true for you too.

Most great companies do many things for free.

The day my air conditioner went out, and I paid a premium for faster service, I didn't feel gouged. I felt served. I felt *grateful*.

I believe you are likely going to heroic lengths to solve problems for your customers, and that if you attached appropriate price tags to those efforts, your customers would not feel gouged. They would feel served. They would feel grateful.

This isn't about seeing what you can get away with. It's about ensuring that you are paid fairly for the excellence you provide to your customers as you take extra measures to solve their problems.

Understanding customers' risk or fear is the first step in solving their problems and will deepen your partnership.

Context matters for price sensitivity. Failing to consider and examine context will cost you opportunities to increase your profit through strategic pricing. It may also cost you an opportunity to be a better partner to your customers. When customers are willing to spend a premium, it often indicates a risk or fear they are trying to mitigate. Understanding that risk or fear is the first step in solving your customers' problems and will deepen your partnership.

Ana the Psychic

Here's another example of variable price sensitivity.

A business owner in Detroit, Jim, told me that he and his wife like to have psychic readings done from time to time, and they have a favorite psychic, Ana. Ana the Psychic books out months in advance for a standard reading, which costs $100.

Jim said that when they want to have a reading, hey don't want to wait months—they want it right away. Ana's rate for an "emergency reading" is $250. So, Jim and his wife will pony up the larger fee for a reading within the week.

There are a lot of reasons I love this story. I don't know Ana the Psychic or the reasons behind her pricing strategy. But I'm going to surmise a few things to illustrate how her approach could help other businesses:

1. Ana the Psychic has created a *segmented pricing strategy* to ensure that she is being paid a premium for services that are of higher value to her clients. "Soon" has higher value than "later." More valuable things can and should be priced higher.

   Where are you adding extra value for customers but failing to charge a premium for it?

2. Again, I'm guessing here, but Ana the Psychic might actually consider the "emergency reading" her desired core offering rather than an exception-based service. She doesn't want to lose out on the most price-sensitive segment of her customers, so she essentially created a discount tier to capture them. (She gives them a big discount but makes them wait at least three months). I suspect Ana's "emergency readings" are more the rule than the exception.

   How can you create segments in your pricing to push customers toward the products and services you prefer to sell? How can you create layers in your pricing to capture all the customers at the highest prices they are willing to pay?

While I am no fan of cost-plus pricing, this strategy has the benefit of making sure Ana the Psychic gets a higher price when her costs are higher. This rests, of course, on my assertion that her human costs of "urgent," short-lead-time work are higher than those of planned, long-lead-time work in the future.

CHAPTER 7

CUSTOMER BUYING CRITERIA

Learning Objectives

1. Identify varying price sensitivities among different customer segments.
2. Understand how focusing on the most price-sensitive customers impacts broader pricing decisions.
3. Explore the need to cater to varying customer priorities beyond price.

Salespeople tend to think of their customers as a homogeneous block: *This is who our customers are, and this is what they care about. This is their buying criteria.*

Companies and sales teams get trapped in making pricing decisions that are too one-size-fits-all based on their most price-sensitive customers. Their decisions about list prices, margin targets, the magnitude of price increases, and so on tend to be overinformed by a few customers. We don't focus on the quiet masses of customers, but instead, we allow the squeaky wheels, the vocal minority, the complainers, and the loud and noisy customers to set our internal barometer for pricing power, market pricing, and pricing confidence. The resulting homogeneous pricing strategy, rooted in the most price-sensitive customers, leaves money on the table.

We know, through our training programs, that salespeople intellectually understand that all customers aren't equally price-sensitive. However, in practical terms, salespeople fall into this mindset trap when they are in the heat of battle, negotiating pricing with customers.

Don't make the mistake of thinking that all customers are the same.

Big Spender or Cheapskate?

To illustrate this idea with audiences, I play a game called "Cheapskate or Big Spender." I have business leaders shout out products or services they value and are willing to spend a price premium ("Big Spender"). I then ask them to call out those items that they don't value as much and are not worth a premium ("Cheapskate"). The resulting list might look something like the below:

Big Spender	Cheapskate
Vacations	Sunglasses
Wine	Bottled Water
Hotels	Coffee
Clothes	Generic Drugs
Toilet Paper	Cars
Coffee	Shampoo
Electronics	Paper Towels
Cars	Wine
Food	Shoes

Glancing at this list, on what items would you spend the extra buck to get the better quality or the better experience?

And when is it overkill to have the fanciest brand or the highest quality?

You might notice something interesting from the lists: some items appear on both sides of the list. These items are both worth a premium and not worth a premium.

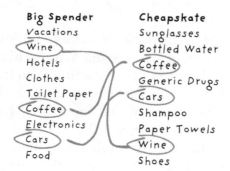

How could that be? How can these items be both worth a premium and not worth a premium?

The answer: We don't place the same priority on the same items. We don't care about the same things the same way, one person to the next.

For example, I prioritize travel and experiences over hard goods. I like to take nice trips and invest my money in meaningful experiences. I don't hesitate to spend a premium for a profound experience. After living there in college, I now take my kids to Spain every couple of years. On the other hand, I drive an inexpensive car. I live in a small home. I rarely shop for clothes, but when I do, I never go to expensive department stores.

My older brother, on the other hand, loves having something tangible to show for the money he spends. He built a 3,000-square-foot heated garage a few years back, and he's always in there, working on his classic car. My brother says my trips to Spain are a waste of money because at the end of two weeks in Spain, I have "nothing to show for it."

So, we have really different ideas about how to spend our money. He's got the garage mahal; I've got a couple of weeks in Spain. Who's the bigger idiot? Well, believe me, arguing about who is the bigger idiot is a lifelong hobby for my brother and me.

But truth be told, I don't think he's an idiot because he can afford that garage. He worked hard for his money, and he got a lot of pleasure and satisfaction from it. While he'd never admit it to me, I don't think he thinks I'm an idiot for taking my kids for a cultural experience that was never available to us when we were kids.

This story has direct applicability in your business because your customers behave in the same way. They spend money on the things important to them, and they have more price sensitivity on the things that aren't. How can your salespeople identify where your customers fall on that spectrum?

Ask them, "Besides price, what else is important to your buying decision?"

Other ways to say this:

"I know pricing will be part of your decision. What else do you care about?"

"Besides the price, what are the other criteria you consider when choosing a supplier?"

"Setting price aside for a moment, what factors are you looking at in your buying process?"

Why phrase the question this way? Because you're asking them to help you understand what factors into their decision *besides price*.

Customers notoriously exaggerate the role that price plays in the buying process. It's in their best interest to do so; telling a salesperson that price is not important gives the salesperson the green light to overcharge.

Even if you hire a third-party firm to investigate your customers' priorities, they will still overreport it. But asking them what *else* is important is a way for your sales team to open up the conversation and discover where to focus their efforts.

> **Ask your customers to help you understand what factors into their decision *besides price*.**

Context Matters

Price sensitivity is not constant by customer, product, service, or even one order to the next.

Not all customers are equally price-sensitive on a given product.

Glidden Paints sells paint and sundries through a number of channels. One of their customer segments is residential repainting contractors—not contractors who paint commercial spaces or even contractors who paint new residential spaces (new home construction). Pretty specific segment, right? But consider that price sensitivity could vary widely over that segment, depending on the customers those contractors serve:

1. Large residential repainting contractors who serve the property-management market, a highly competitive and largely commoditized industry where speed matters most

2. Small, specialty residential painters who might spend four days painting a metallic faux finish on the Jones family bathroom

Both segments use paint brushes for cutting in corners, ceilings, trim, and so on. Who is more sensitive about the price of these brushes? The large commercial contractor. Same product. Different sensitivity.

The same customer buying the same product or service may not be equally price-sensitive on every order.

One of my clients, an office furniture distributor, provides furniture design, distribution, and installation services for commercial interiors and office spaces. Most of their business is bid-based and highly competitive. Often, they must price low to win large jobs.

Suppose this distributor wins a bid to furnish a space containing one hundred workstations at 18 percent gross margin. If their customer wants to add three workstations six months later, should the distributor supply them at the same 18 percent margin? No, and they don't. Nor is the customer surprised by it (although they will still try to get lower pricing), understanding the volume discount of the original order. Same customer, same products, same services. Different sensitivity.

Our Most Price-Sensitive Customers Limit Our Thinking

You may be thinking, *We know our customers have different price sensitivities. We segment our customers.* Because of your granular segmentation, you may think that you don't fall prey to one-size-fits-all pricing decision-making.

Let me challenge you on this: Pick one slice of your customers, the narrowest slice you can—say, large OEMs on the West Coast who buy over a million dollars. What are the buying criteria for that kind of customer? What's important to them?

If you were to make a list of priorities for that segment of your customers, price would be on the list, but so might quality, service, relationship, speed, inventory, ability to meet deadlines, and more. If you made that list, it would be the right list because you know your customers.

Now, if I took that list to all the customers inside that slice and said, "Is this what you care about when you're choosing between this company and their competitor?" they'd say, "Yes, that's what I care about." If I said, "Scratch out anything you can live without," they'd say, "I can't. All are important." But if I asked all these customers to order the list by importance, none of those customers would put the list in the same order.

Some customers would put price right at the top, and if you are a nickel more, you're out. You have other customers for whom service, quality, speed, or inventory would top the list. (Of course, even for the customer who puts price at the bottom, you still have to be in a competitive range.)

For the customer who puts price at the top, your pricing power is more limited. But what about for that customer who cares more about service, quality, and speed—all things you excel at as a company? How much pricing power do you have with them? Much more.

I'm not saying that if you are great and the customer values other things over price you can charge anything you want. Even if you make the world's best raisin bread, you can't charge $150 per loaf. There are limits to the range of pricing, but I'd like to see your pricing at the top of that range for the customers that value other factors over price.

Generally, that kind of super segmentation and price granularity don't happen. We think something like "$X is a good price for a large OEM on the West Coast buying over $1 million."

The most price-sensitive customers limit your thinking.

The problem with thinking of your customers (or a segment of your customers) as a monolithic block is that your most price-sensitive customers become the archetype. The "lowest common denominator," in the form of price bullies, sets your baseline for "market price." We start thinking things like *X is a good price for this kind of SKU. Y is a good margin for this kind of project. Z is pretty good pricing for this kind of work.* But X, Y, and Z are rules of thumb developed around your most price-sensitive customers.

The most price-sensitive customers limit your thinking. The more homogeneous you are, the less money you make

The riches are in the niches!

because it's always the most price-sensitive customers that drive our pricing confidence and rules of thumb.

Get ever more granular in your pricing approach because the more granular we are, the more money we make. The more homogeneous and one-size-fits-all we are, the less money we make. Because even within a very small slice of our business, not all those customers care about price the same way. The riches are in the niches!

Let's look at Foundry Metals, a company that manufactures machined steel and aluminum parts across many industries. They knew their customers cared about quality, on-time in-full (OTIF) delivery, and price as their primary criteria. And yes, *all* of their customers wanted high quality, 100 percent on-time, in-full delivery, and low prices. But all customers don't care about all of those things equally:

- One of their customer segments was the oil and gas industry, which used their parts in offshore drilling. For this industry, unplanned downtime for any reason costs them thousands of dollars per minute of lost drilling time. Quality and reliability were, by far, the most important considerations for this industry.

- Foundry also sold some parts through distributors, whose primary considerations were price and OTIF delivery. Those distributors, in turn, sold to contractors in the HVAC and vacuum industries, who cared about quality, but the stakes were much lower than the off-shore drilling applications. Price played a bigger role in their decisions.

Rather than set one-size-fits-all pricing and margin targets for their products regardless of customer need, creating a more granular pricing strategy was the key to Foundry's successful pursuit of higher profits while remaining competitive in the most price-sensitive segments of customers.

Key Takeaways

- Customers within the same segment can have vastly different price sensitivities.
- Overemphasis on price-sensitive customers can lead to a homogenized, less effective pricing approach.
- Sales teams need to probe beyond price to understand other critical buying criteria.
- Segmenting customers based on their buying criteria can lead to more targeted pricing approaches.
- Avoiding a one-size-fits-all pricing strategy is crucial for maximizing revenue.
- Training sales teams to engage customers about their specific needs and values can enhance pricing effectiveness.

Client Spotlight: Brad Tinney, Birmingham Fastener

There is no *one right time* to increase prices. For family-owned manufacturer and distributor Birmingham Fastener, the right time was in the midst of the pandemic.

The company typically spent around $150,000 a year on trade shows, but with shows canceled due to COVID-19, they saw an opportunity to transform their business. CEO Brad Tinney recalls, "We said, 'Let's take a portion of that trade show budget and turn it into continuous improvement and training... Our salespeople can't get out and call on customers right now. Let's take this opportunity and turn it into a positive.'"

Tinney signed his team up for Boost's Pricing Power Series. Their goal was to establish a cohesive pricing approach for more than 80 salespeople in 22 locations across the country.

"It forced us to get deep into our probably 2,800 active customers," Tinney says. "Grading those customers and getting down to some of those not in the top 20 percent." Segmenting their customers—applying different pricing strategies based on customer type and volume—allowed them to raise prices where they would make the biggest impact, particularly on those "hot sauce" items where they were industry leaders.

Over time, Tinney says, "I literally watched our gross margins go up, double-digit—10, 12, 13 percent"—across various product lines.

Tinney also attributes a lasting cultural transformation at Birmingham Fastener to the training. And he didn't just send his salespeople through the program—he was an active participant in and contributor to the first wave of training.

"I love getting to teach our salespeople—who would typically give away the farm—the tools that they need to have, the right words to say when somebody across the desk or somebody on the other side of the line compares them to someone else," Tinney says. "We need to get paid for doing things that no one in the land can do and not have any guilt, any remorse, to know that we're investing back in our companies and our people."

The training instilled a deep sense of pride and confidence in the sales team. They learned how to stand firm in negotiations and articulate the value of their products and services. This cultural shift empowered them to turn down unreasonable demands and maintain profitable pricing.

Tinney says that not only was the Boost training one of the highest ROI investments he's ever made at Birmingham Fastener, but it also reaped benefits for the company in unifying their salespeople and solidifying their value in the marketplace.

"It's just a confidence to stand up for who we are and what we believe in," Tinney says. "We provide great products and great services, but we expect to be compensated for that. And if you're a good partner, you're a good customer of ours; you want us to be here tomorrow. You want us to be here the day after that."

CHAPTER 8

IDENTIFYING THE HOT SAUCE

Learning Objectives

1. Explore how margin memory ruts or pricing memory ruts influence pricing discussions.
2. Identify low-sensitivity products in your portfolio for potential pricing improvement.
3. Learn to challenge established pricing norms and pricing "rules of thumb" to uncover new revenue opportunities.

I can make a roomful of business owners change their minds about their pricing power with a simple game that takes two minutes.

First, I ask, "What's the current price for a gallon of regular unleaded gasoline?"

Every time, they come within a few pennies of the right answer. Everyone knows the price of gasoline.

Then, I ask: "What's the current price for a 6-ounce bottle of Texas Pete's Hot Sauce?"

This time, no one answers. Their silence begs another question: "Who cares?" And that's the point. We don't know the price of hot sauce because it's beneath our notice.

Why do we know so much about the price of gas and so little about the price of hot sauce?

We know the gas price because we buy it all the time, filling up our tanks once or twice a week. If the price goes up a lot, we all notice it, talk about it, and see it in the news. The price of gas has a noticeable effect on our personal finances.

If the price of hot sauce goes up a lot, no one knows. We might buy it once a year. If we run out, we just go to the store and buy more. If it's $1 or $6, it makes no difference to our personal finances. We just throw it in the cart and move on without a second thought.

Most businesses have hot sauce and gasoline in their portfolio of products and services, but we think of everything as gas. We think that if we raise our prices and hold the line on discounts, our customers will leave us—and perhaps that's somewhat true, but it's far truer for our gasoline products and services than for our "hot sauce."

Most businesses have hot sauce and gasoline in their portfolio of products and services, but we think of everything as gas.

We're so close to our own business that everything looks like gasoline to us, but it doesn't all look like gasoline to our customers. Some things are hot sauce—throw them in the cart and move on.

Which Products and Services Are Least Sensitive?

I'll illustrate this with a story about one of the office furniture dealers I worked with, C&M Office Interiors. I presented this information to them, and they said, "Okay, we get this, but our industry is so competitive, so commoditized, that everything we sell is gasoline. Tons of bloody-knuckle price discussions, a lot of bid-based work, razor-thin margins. *Everything* we sell is gas."

I said, "Hang on a second. You mean to tell me you're putting, say, 20 items on a quote, or 200, or 2,000, and every single item is getting the same amount of scrutiny and attention?"

We went back and forth, and where we landed is that only tables, chairs, cubicle walls, filing cabinets, and desks get that intense price scrutiny from their customers. Those are the most price-sensitive items they sell—the center of their business. Accessory products like in/out trays, telephone caddies, wastepaper cans, monitor arms, sound masking, fabric protection, and artwork are less sensitive.

For example, on a recent highly competitive deal, C&M "had to" be at a 14, meaning a 14 percent gross profit. What they'd done is put every single item on the quote at 14 percent gross profit. They put 18 percent on their core products—the tables, chairs, desks—*and* on their accessory products alike.

I said, "If you have to be at 14 percent on these core items, that's fine, but you don't have to be at 14 percent on the accessories. Could you be at 24, or 18, or 14.2—anything more than 14?"

They replied that accessories make up only 10 percent of their volume. A 10 percent increase on 10 percent of the volume results in a 1 percent price lift, which would double their profitability. (They started with 1 percent net profit. Increasing pricing by 1 percent moved their net profit to 2 percent, a 100 percent lift!)

The lesson: do not ignore the opportunity to take a price increase in the fringes of your business. It's often where you have the biggest opportunity.

You may say, "Oh, we're not that blunt. We already price our gasoline and our hot sauce products differently." But are your prices different *enough*? Is there a chance that the price sensitivity around your gasoline limits your thinking on the hot sauce? Are you pricing your hot sauce only slightly higher than the gasoline when you could go much higher?

> Do not ignore the opportunity to take a price increase in the fringes of your business. It's often where you have the biggest opportunity.

We're so close to our own businesses, and we spend most of our time thinking about gasoline because that's where the demand is. That's where all the market intel and price pushback are, which set our idea of pricing and "what the market will bear." From that vantage point, we look at the hot sauce, see a 10-point price premium, and think, "That looks darn good from here!" But that's only good if that 10-point premium couldn't be 15 or 25.

Often, we constrain the profitability of the hot sauce because of the limits of our own thinking. But we have to interrogate our own thinking, inspect our own beliefs, and break our rules. Is the price ceiling on hot sauce of our own creation?

To illustrate this idea, here's another related story from C&M. One of their products was a $3,000 cubicle system, and they sold proprietary bracketry that went with it for

$0.97. I asked them, "Why not $1.47 for this hardware? Why not $2.47? Why not $3.97? You have to get your heads around this hot sauce concept!"

One of the salespeople said, "But that's 90 percent margin!" I replied, "Your customers do not know or care what your margin is!"

Let me say that again because it's really important: No one cares about your margins.

Your customers don't call you up and say, "This quote is a little expensive. What else do you have more in the 22 percent margin range?" But I often hear teams talking about margins like that is *the* thing that determines customers' willingness to pay. It's a proxy for price. But it's not the same thing.

No one cares about your margins.

Sometimes, salespeople tell us they could never charge X amount because it's "too much profit." They have a mental limit on how much margin is acceptable. That "acceptable" price or margin window is informed by their past selling experiences. (Not only does the office furniture customer not care about paying 90 percent margin, but they are also not worried about the price of a bracket that costs a couple of bucks when they're buying a $3,000 cubicle system.)

We tend to have rules of thumb in our business. For example, a salesperson operates with a rule of thumb that 20 percent is a competitive margin, 30 percent is great, but 40 percent rips someone off. He can't imagine a world in which this hot sauce item could possibly be sold at a 90 percent margin. He has a self-imposed cap on pricing and margin.

Take the cap off your hot sauce pricing. I trust that you have intimate knowledge about the market pricing of your gasoline, but you get far less feedback on the pricing of your hot sauce. Be willing to push that a little bit.

Where do you have margin memory or pricing memory? Where do pricing ruts hold you back? Your salespeople made up these rules of thumb. Yes, they are informed by selling experience, but nonetheless fallible, and you shouldn't take them as facts. These rules live in their heads, holding them back. Just as I shared in Chapter 7 about pricing granularity by customer, we must be more granular in pricing by product and service. Remember, the riches are in the niches!

Here's something to try with your team: Have each salesperson gather five recent invoices and review them together. Go line by line and talk about each price. Circle at least one line item on each invoice where you know customers aren't as sensitive and you could consider increasing the price. (This advice isn't just for companies selling products; service-based businesses have hot sauce, too!)

Which Wraparound Charges Can Be Increased?

Sometimes the hot sauce isn't even the products or services you sell but, instead, the charges you wrap around those products and services. For the office furniture dealer, another win came from one such wraparound charge: freight.

On an invoice for $50,000 worth of office furniture, the last line item was a freight fee of $300. I knew it was hot sauce, so I told them to double it. Their salespeople *freaked out*. All their customer "data" indicated they were price-sensitive on *everything*.

I knew, however, that the office furniture was the gasoline—that was what their customers were paying attention to. That was where they were being heavily evaluated, certainly on price, but also on whether the product met the spec, post-sale service, installation quality, and design aesthetic.

So, I recommended a 100 percent price increase in one of the most competitive and commoditized industries I have ever consulted in. Three hundred dollars for a truck charge is *hot sauce*—throw it in the cart and move on. No one was choosing them over the competition based on that item.

The salespeople wanted to argue with me over this, and I argued right back: "Try this on three deals. You can waive it, roll it back, and call me and tell me I'm dead wrong, but please try it." That I'm including this story gives away the ending. Their standard truck charge has been $600 ever since. I called them up a few years later and asked, "How's it going with the truck charge?" They replied, "It's good; no one ever says anything about it."

So, I told them, "DOUBLE IT AGAIN!"

If you do not sell a physical product to ship, or if freight is highly price-sensitive for your customers, then freight is not your opportunity. But there is something like this in your business. *What are people not paying attention to? What wraparound charges, such as environmental fees, document fees, disposal fees, or ancillary fees could you increase without pushback?*

What Are You Not Charging That You Could Charge?

I showed C&M Office Interiors how to identify products, services, and wraparound charges that were less sensitive for their customers. The last thing I asked was, "What are you not getting paid for?"

You have another opportunity—where you aren't charging for things that come along for free with the products and services you sell. Where do you expend time and effort that doesn't generate revenue? What could be a revenue stream that is not today?

Where do you expend time and effort that could become a revenue stream?

I broke them into teams and said, "We're going to play the 'Nickel and Dime Game.'" The idea is that if you were going to nickel-and-dime your customers to death, what's everything you could bill them for?

I added a bonus challenge to the "Nickel and Dime Game," asking them to consider where else they were leaking profit through sub-optimized pricing. I asked, "Where are your policies, processes, and pricing not tuned to capture maximum profits for our value?" These profit leaks are "holes in your pocket" and include various types of discounting, free or underpriced services, unenforced policies, or other leaks.

They brainstormed, and together we generated a list of 87 items they could charge for.

As we were creating this list, I watched as the anxiety of the salespeople in the room went up. "If we charged for all these things," one salesperson told me, "We'd be out of business in a month!" I said, "Oh, I don't think it would take that long."

You can't implement all 87 charges. The key is to play the game full out, get all the ideas on the board, and then pick the *one or two* of the most sensible, defensible, and least visible items that will actually generate revenue, and leave the other 85 things free, reminding yourself in the process of all that you do for free that your competition does not do at all or as well as you do.

This is important because your company does a lot of things for your customers for free. You're going to heroic lengths to solve problems for your customers, to make their lives easier, and you're not attaching a price tag to it when you could. (And when you should.)

You do this because you're professional, you're great at what you do, and it's easy for you. It's part of your culture to show up, put your shoulder to the wheel, and work hard

You're going to heroic lengths to solve problems for your customers for free.

for your customers. You don't even think about it, and you start taking it for granted. But if you take it for granted, guess who else takes it for granted? *Your customers do.*

When they take your excellence for granted, they use up your resources without any regard for how that impacts your business. This is not usually done with malice; it's just a natural occurrence of this truth: *what is free is abused.* If we don't charge for something, we're telling the customer it's not worth anything, and they ascribe no value to it. An example of this comes again from the office furniture industry.

For years, these companies would offer design work for free if you bought their products. These companies had teams of talented and experienced creatives doing design work based on what the customer wanted. But what would happen when the customer came back and wanted to put an atrium in the middle? How many

If we don't charge for something, we're telling the customer it's not worth anything, and they ascribe no value to it.

rounds of revisions would the designers go through *for free?*

Until you have boundaries that cost customers, they will take advantage of you. They will abuse what is free. For the office furniture dealer, that might look like offering the first two rounds of designs for free and then charging an hourly rate for every revision after that.

One takeaway here is you can use pricing to drive better customer behavior. In our example, if the customer knows they have to pay for more work, that might motivate them to make their decisions within a certain timeframe and in fewer rounds. And if they don't, they will pay for the choice to work outside your normal processes.

Even if you decide not to charge for *any* of the freebies your team identifies in the Nickel and Dime Game, the exercise will remind you of the value you're giving your customers that they aren't getting from your competitors. And then, you can start to message on these free benefits—using this offensively and defensively to prevent and respond to price objections. It's likely you stopped selling on those points when you started taking them for granted.

The goal is to identify where you are incurring time and effort but not getting paid for it. Play the Nickel and Dime Game in your organization, and you'll be surprised by what you learn about all the special ways you're taking care of customers, even if you don't decide to charge for them.

I presented this idea to the sales team of an industrial caster manufacturer that sells to the auto industry's big three, but also to tier-one and tier-two automotive suppliers and a variety of other industrial environments. As we were playing the Nickel and Dime Game, one person in the audience kept saying, "Ford would never pay us that. Ford would never go for that. Ford would put us out to bid immediately if we tried that."

Well, guess what? Ford is one of the largest, most powerful, most aggressive purchasing engines in the world. They don't want to pay anyone for anything ever, and they're pretty good at pulling that off. I asked him how many customers they had—611 active customers. I asked how many of those 611 were not Ford. Do not extrapolate Ford's price sensitivity to the rest of your customers. Just because you can't charge it everywhere doesn't mean you can't charge it anywhere.

Don't make the mistake of letting your entire price strategy be dictated by your most price-sensitive customers.

You may have a "Ford" in your customer base who will never pay more. But what about the other 99 customers who *will* pay more? Don't make the mistake of letting your entire price strategy be dictated by your most price-sensitive customers.

Nickel and Dime Game

Play the Nickel and Dime with your team to uncover opportunities to increase profitability by capturing value that is currently free or underpriced.

1. **Free:** Brainstorm every possible fee, surcharge, or additional service that could have been charged for but wasn't (e.g., rush fees, delivery fees, restocking fees).

2. **Underpriced:** Identify products, services, project types, fees and surcharges, and so on that you charge for today but that may be underpriced. This is an opportunity to identify "hot sauce," overlooked, less visible products and services to drive profits without intense customer scrutiny or pushback.

Prioritize opportunities based on anticipated customer response, feasibility, and expected impact on profitability. Select a small number of sensible and defensible charges to implement.

WORKSHEET | NICKEL – DIME GAME

Here's an example of the worksheet completed by the service division of one of our manufacturing clients:

WORKSHEET | NICKEL – DIME GAME

Charge for Stamping
Charge for Banding
Charge for Trailer Overnight
Driver Redelivery Fee
Rush Service
Charge More for Storage
Protection Fee/Insurance
Retooling Fee
Reduce Volume Discounts
Reduce Rebates
Small Order Charge/Setup Fee
Charge Restocking Fee
Increase Handling Fees
Service Fee (New Problem, Same Equipment)
Avoid Unbilled Time / Create Change Orders
Stop Honoring Quotes Past Expiry Date
Start Enforcing Current Return Policy
Receiving, Cross-Dock, and Storage Fees
Lock out Price Overrides (Require Approval)
Multiple Trip Charge if Customer-Driven
Pass Along Manufacturer's Increase
Adjust Payment Terms
Custom Size Fee
Verify New Pricing in System
Mark Up Freight
Eliminate All XWX7's from the System

Download a fillable PDF of the Nickel-Dime Game Worksheet here:

Where's Your Hot Sauce?

In the last chapter, I showed how your most price-sensitive customers limit your thinking. The same thing happens with your products and services. Your most price-sensitive products and services hold your salespeople back from increasing the price of your less sensitive items.

Combat this by identifying your hot sauce and play the Nickel and Dime Game. To do this, you and your sales team have to ask yourselves the following questions:

1. To what products and services are our customers paying less attention? How can we increase our prices on those items?
2. What surcharges and wraparound fees already included in our invoices could we increase?
3. What are we not charging for that we could charge for?
4. Where are our processes, policies, and pricing sub-optimized for maximum profitability for value?

Examine your business through this lens, and you will see opportunities to revisit your pricing, whether it's with certain customers or customer segments, on specific products and services, or on those many free things you do for your customers they could pay for.

Key Takeaways

- Businesses often have highly price-sensitive (gasoline) and less sensitive (hot sauce) products and services.

- Recognizing which products and services are less price-sensitive can guide strategic price increases and ad hoc pricing opportunities.

- Reevaluating wraparound fees and ancillary charges can unlock incremental margin.

- Challenging traditional margin perceptions can lead to more profitable pricing decisions.

- Sales teams need to understand that customers don't know or care about margins.

- The Nickel and Dime Game helps identify previously overlooked revenue opportunities and reveals how much value-added service is given away.

- Incremental charges for additional services can generate revenue and manage customer expectations.

Client Spotlight: Matt Crenshaw, Nova

One of the biggest challenges with price increases is that companies don't do them often enough.

Matt Crenshaw is the CEO of Nova, a B2B software company making digital advertising easier through creative automation. Their clients range from big media companies to technology platforms and digital ad agencies.

Despite the variety in their clients, Nova had a fairly simple rate card. However, it was *too* simple. They hadn't updated it in years.

"We had gotten used to our pricing. Everyone on our team knew it by heart," says Crenshaw, whose company operates on a usage-based pricing model. "We were speaking in round numbers, which felt hard to move away from."

Working with Boost, Crenshaw was convinced of the power of small, incremental changes to pricing.

Crenshaw and Nova's head of sales took a fresh look at the company's rate card. As they discussed various options for price increases, they took a more nuanced approach to each of their major accounts. In some cases, opportunities arose to consider entirely new pricing models—a win for Nova and some of its partners.

Crenshaw says that one of the most advantageous shifts for Nova in this process was focusing on the *execution* of the price increase and not treating it as an overly academic strategy project.

"So often, companies run an elaborate pricing strategy project and generate these huge research reports. Their board reviews it and loves it because boards know the value of price increases. But then it goes to the sales team and gathers dust in someone's desk drawer," Crenshaw says.

Nova worked with Boost to develop a systematic approach to rolling out its price increases, giving its sales team templates and talking points, and tracking the results closely.

These small price increases, when executed regularly, can yield big benefits as prices begin to compound over time.

"Pricing is like going to the gym," says Crenshaw. "You have to sort of revisit it and do it over and over and over again and get your reps in. It can't be something you do once, cross off the list, and then revisit the next time somebody screams about it."

PART 4

PRICING FOR VALUE

Your salespeople have unexercised pricing power in two main areas: where your customers aren't paying attention and where you're underpriced relative to your value. In Part 3, we looked at how to find riches in the niches—where your customers aren't paying attention—and now, we'll look at how to lower their sensitivity by pricing appropriately for the extraordinary value you provide.

Pricing for value means ensuring that the messaging you wrap around your sales process helps you extract the highest price for the value you deliver to your customers.

What your customer hopes to get out of their buying process is the best product or service—at the worst guy's price. This is what's behind the "Can't Hurt to Ask" club. This is what's behind all those other tactics your customers use when they're trying to get the best deal from you.

Of course, trying to get the best deal through tactics and negotiation is rational and prepared purchasing behavior. So, what can the rational and prepared seller do? Two things are essential to being paid well for value in the face of these tactics:

1. **Deliver excellence.** Of course, you must deliver on your brand promise. Be who your customers count on you to be. Own and resolve mistakes.

2. **Reduce the importance of price in the buying process.** Make price fade to the background as a secondary consideration. We talked, in Chapter 7, about customers' lists of buying criteria; our purpose in value selling is to make price a *lesser* consideration than other criteria. (For a customer who values low price above all else, if your salespeople can pull price down to number two on the list, that is a massive victory in value selling.)

In Part 4, I'll take you through examples of companies that have done an excellent job of this. These businesses were able to lower their customers' price sensitivity in one of six ways:

1. By focusing on *why* the customer is buying
2. By solving a unique problem for their customers, making price a lesser consideration
3. By avoiding the mistake of signaling low quality with their pricing
4. By formulating and practicing the most effective responses to customers' price objections

5. By illuminating the true cost of choosing an inferior option

6. By compelling customers to reveal what they truly value through offered options

Don't Wait for Perfection

I shared above that your customers' goal is to buy the best product or service available at the worst competitor's price. When I share this with sales teams, sometimes they get hung up on the word *best*. When I say that, I mean best-in-class or better-in-class; I *don't* mean perfect.

Sometimes, sales teams point a finger at some operational problem and use that as an excuse to procrastinate on taking a position of greater price leadership. You may be reading this and thinking, *We can't be a price leader. We had an inventory blip last November and some team turnover in April. We need to wait until we get our operational house in order before we can think about a price increase.*

I would like to disabuse you of the notion that you need to be operationally perfect to take price in the market. Operational perfection does not exist in the marketplace—not for you, not for your competitors, not for your customers. If you wait for the day when you're perfect in your delivery of your products and services to ask for higher prices, you are abdicating the opportunity to be paid what you are worth *right now*.

Of course, if your business is operationally troubled—if you can't fill any orders, or the phone is ringing off the hook with angry customers, or, worse yet, the phone isn't ringing at all because no one wants to buy from you—that is a different story. If you are in a disastrous situation, now isn't the time for price improvement; it's the time to right the ship operationally.

But if you deliver on your brand promise, if you clean up messes when you make them and stand behind your work, then you have an opportunity to ask for more. More than an opportunity—I would say you have a *responsibility* for price leadership. Don't wait for perfection. Don't let yourselves or your teams off the hook like that.

Get Paid for Your Excellence: A Story to Inspire You

Once upon a time, Pablo Picasso was sketching in a plaza, and a woman recognized him and asked him to sketch her. He agreed to do so and dashed off a quick sketch.

When she saw the sketch, she was so fascinated by how well he captured her spirit, her je ne sais quoi, that she asked him if he would sell her the sketch. He quoted her a price of 5,000 francs, a considerable sum of money for that time.

The woman was surprised and, in fact, outraged. She said to him, "But sir, it only took you five minutes." And he replied, "No, madame. It took me a lifetime."

Why is this story relevant? As a business owner, you and your teams are experts at what you do, deeply masterful in your craft. You have deep expertise in your business, resident in the products and services you deliver and how you deliver them. And when you are truly masterful, the work gets easy. It gets fast. It's a piece of cake. *Becoming* an expert is hard, but once you *are* an expert, it's easy. It stops looking special to you or to your team.

For example, have you ever had a customer come to you with an "unsolvable" problem, only for you to see, almost immediately, the best way to tackle it? The only reason you can solve it, and so quickly, is that you've done it a thousand times before. If you've ever thought, *No problem, the team can knock out that extra task in under two hours,* consider this: the only reason the team can do the work so quickly is because they've done it a thousand times before.

But just because you're good at something and you can do it quickly and well doesn't mean it's not worth a premium. You know the work it took to get your business to this point of expertise. And that expertise is what allows you to provide a premium product or service. It would take your customers ten times as long to do, and it would be a tenth as good—if they could create it at all. (The same goes for your less qualified competition.)

Do not be tempted to underprice what is valuable to the customer just because it happens to be easy or fast for you to produce; it's no less valuable to them. And remember: They are not paying you for your time; they're paying you for your brilliance.

> Just because you're good at something and you can do it quickly and well doesn't mean it's not worth a premium.

You're Picasso, baby. Get paid.

CHAPTER 9

WHY THEY BUY

Learning Objectives

1. Learn techniques to logically convince and emotionally persuade customers of your value proposition to justify higher prices.
2. Understand the critical role that buyer emotions play in the sales process and authentically connect with customers' emotional needs to drive sales. Explore and leverage the utility of positive and negative emotions.
3. Learn to employ the Feature-Advantage-Benefit Matrix to sell value, not features.

The phrase "Sell the sizzle, not the steak" was coined in 1936 by Elmer Wheeler, head of the Tested Selling Institute and author of *Tested Sentences That Sell.* Wheeler developed selling sentences for over 5,000 products that focused not on the products' features but on how the products helped the customer.

Wheeler also coined the following selling sentence for Barbasol shaving cream: "How would you like to cut your shaving time in half?" This masterful marketing phrase, which focused not on the product but instead on the customer, boosted sales of shaving cream 300 percent.

The lesson in this approach is clear: Focus less on selling the features of your solution and sell instead from the point of view of the customer. What's in it for them? Turn the entire sales process toward the problems you solve for customers, the goals you help them realize, the pain points that address, and the dreams you help come true.

Feature selling is about you. You'll struggle to sell at a price premium if you sell this way.

Value selling is about the customer. By connecting to the real issues customers face, you make price less important in the customer's buying process.

Have you ever spent time with someone who went on and on about themselves? It's no fun. And when you talk with your customers endlessly about the features of your solution, you are subjecting them to a very similar routine.

Instead, use the customer's pain points to understand how best to position your solution. Use their frustrations and headaches and fears about their current solution and provider. Or connect with the wild enthusiasm they feel about the possibilities. In other words, connect with the customer's deeper emotions that live *beneath* this purchase. Get in the hearts and minds of the customer by using the customer's language.

Here's another example: Charles Revson, who co-founded the Revlon company in 1932 and ran it for 43 years, said, "In the factory, we manufacture cosmetics; in the store, we sell hope."

This statement is brilliant. Why? One of Revlon's top-selling products is lipstick. Lipstick is pigmented grease rolled in a tube. When a person walks into Sephora and throws down $35 for a lipstick, it's not because they want to own a tube of pigmented grease. They buy lipstick because when they wear it, they feel confident and beautiful.

We focus so much on what we sell. Where we need to focus is on *why* the customer buys.

What does lipstick have to do with successfully negotiating higher prices for your products and services? No matter what you sell, the reason people buy is because of the *problem it solves*. None of your customers, not one of them, woke up excited to give you a big check for your product or service. They woke up excited to have their problem solved.

We focus so much on *what* we sell. We become feature-focused in our sales messaging: *Let me tell you about the proprietary emollients of our pigmented grease.* Where we need to focus is on *why* the customer buys. And please: focus on the logical reasons as well as the emotional reasons to buy. (Selling at premium prices is about hearts *and* minds!)

I'm not saying you shouldn't share your solution's features with customers. Especially when selling more technical products and services to knowledgeable buyers, diving deeply into the features is generally necessary. But don't stop there. Explore the emotional ramifications. The headaches you solve for them, the risks you help them avoid, the pain points you solve, or the hopes and dreams you can help them connect to—that is the space of price premium.

Have you heard the marketing statement "No one wants to buy a quarter-inch drill; they want to buy a quarter-inch hole?" There's not a store in the world where you can buy a quarter-inch hole. You have to buy the drill. And if you're in the business of selling drills, you want to show everyone all the great features of your drill. But what does the customer *need*? A hole. Sell them the hole. Sell them the hole they already want, and then, sell them the perfect drill for that hole.

> **Connect with the customers' problem, pain, fear, dream, or vision to earn a price premium.**

Customers don't buy features. They buy to solve a problem; connect with that pain, that fear, that dream, that vision to earn a price premium.

Don't Talk about *Your* Features, Talk about *Their* Value

Don't confuse feature selling (all about you) with value selling (all about the customer). Here's the difference:

"Our widget is made from a high-quality titanium alloy. It is 25 percent more reliable than the competitor's product. Our programmable controls allow you to select up to seven different pressure settings. Also, we are a family-owned business and have been in business for 37 years. Buy my widget for $300."

Who is this statement about? You! The seller. It's focused on the features of *your* product and *your* business. Do you want to close more sales at higher prices? Focus on the customer! What problem do they have? What is their pain point? What makes them tick? Value selling focuses on the value of your product or service in the context of the *customer's* needs, wants, desires, fears, and so on.

Try this instead:

"When your production line goes down because of a widget failure, it can cost you over $1,000 per hour in lost production. Our higher quality materials and much higher reliability mean far less downtime for you. With our widget, you can avoid up to $14,000 per month in unplanned production stoppages. At $380, this part pays for itself in just a couple of days! Also, because you can finely tune the pressure to the exact dispensing rate you require, you waste far less raw material by using our widget."

See the difference? The second statement is all about the customer and their needs. It's the same widget with the same features described in the first statement, but it's described in the language and the context of what the customer values. When you solve the customer's problems, price fades from the place of highest importance to the background. Suddenly, $380 looks like a bargain to the customer, even though the competitor's inferior product is only $300.

I built this example on a widget, but the same principle holds true when you are selling services. Consider an engineering firm that shared this list with me as their compelling value proposition:

- We are internationally recognized as a leader in designing, deploying, and supporting tanker fuel infrastructure systems and delivery programs.
- We are an experienced team with more than 20 PhD engineers on staff. Our staff has an average of 18 years of industry experience, with 10 senior engineers and 40 years of industry experience.

- Our engineers helped to develop industry standards and regulations, and we have co-authored over a dozen articles on fuel deployment.
- Since our founding, we have been involved in the National Petroleum Institute, through which we led a joint industry project on fuel infrastructure deployment.
- We developed a state-of-the-art assessment methodology that allows us to account for in-service degradation.

But talking about the credentials of their people, their experience and training, and so on doesn't help the customer understand how this firm will better meet their particular needs. How do these features translate to benefits in the areas of improved profit, revenue growth, asset protection, risk, customer satisfaction, and safety? And then, how do those benefits tie to the emotional impact on the customer? Get specific about how your service solves the customers' problems. Clarify why they should care, and you will have a much easier time winning work at higher prices.

When you get specific about how the features of your products and services solve the customer's problem, then you are value selling. When you sell on value, price becomes a secondary or tertiary consideration.

Goals and Hopes, or Costs and Frustrations?

You can connect to the emotional needs of your customer through positive or negative emotions:

- Where does your product or service create excitement and enthusiasm? Where does your solution serve your customers' goals, visions, ambitions, and dreams?

- What fear, pain, doubt, and worries does your product or service solve? How can your solution prevent customer headaches and disappointment?

Both approaches are appropriate, reasonable, and useful.

So, should you go negative? Research shows that negative emotions drive decision-making to a larger degree and with more urgency than positive emotions because of something called negativity bias, which we introduced in Chapter 5. Negativity bias is our tendency to

- react more intensely to negative stimuli than to equally positive stimuli.
- recall negative events more strongly than positive events.

A tendency to overemphasize the negative can impact your customers' buying decisions. To capitalize on the negativity bias, tap into the negative emotional impact on your customer's current situation. How can your solution help them? Uncover their concerns, fears, and worries, and then connect to this emotional need to drive the sale.

Tapping into the customer's fear and worry is, often, a more effective sales technique and drives more urgent decision making. Of course, it's not always the right tactic. Carefully consider what the customer cares about and what approach is most appropriate.

And, if you choose to explore the negative emotional role in the customer's decision process, be authentic and empathetic. This isn't about scare tactics or manipulation.

If you cannot authentically address a customer's pain point with your solution, then selling this way is manipulative, dangerous, and even unethical. Customers can sniff out your inauthenticity, which will critically damage their trust in you. You must come from a place of true customer service to sell this way effectively.

What About Buyers Who "Only Care About Price?"

If you think the principles of this chapter don't apply when dealing with procurement agents and professional buyers who "only care about price," you're wrong. Spoiler alert: procurement professionals and corporate buyers are humans too. They are not immune to their emotions playing a role in their decision-making.

Remember, price is never the *only* consideration. Often, it's not even the most important, even to procurement professionals.

The best salespeople use the knowledge that emotions affect buying decisions to get at what buyers really care about. Price will always be on the list; it will always be a factor. But what *else* is on the list?

What would the boss say if the buyer chooses a vendor that cuts corners on quality just to save a buck? What if the buyer chooses a cheaper supplier that can't deliver on time? No one wants to be chewed out, or worse. On the positive side, how can the buyer be the hero of the organization by making sure that quality is exceptional, delivery is fast, and supply is stable? Procurement people want to ensure that the products and services they buy satisfy the business leaders and operational teams. If you are selling to a procurement professional, how can you be the easiest to buy from, the one who lowers her risk, the one who makes her look good, the one who saves her time and hassle?

There's always a *why* beyond price.

Type I and Type II Thinking

Research from behavioral psychology supports the notion that human beings are not as logical as we might imagine. Two thought processes work in our brains when we make decisions:

- **Type I** is intuitive, subconscious, emotionally driven, and fast.
- **Type II** is analytical, rational, and much slower.

Type II thinking helps us justify our decisions, but increasingly, research suggests that Type I thinking has far more influence on how we make decisions in the first place. We decide on emotion and justify those decisions afterward with facts.

Does this emotional, gut-driven decision-making extend to the business world? Does it extend to the B2B sales and procurement arenas? Emphatically, yes. Check out these shocking stats:

50%	BUYING DECISIONS IN B2B DRIVEN BY EMOTION
65%	SUBJECTIVE FACTORS INCREASINGLY MATTER WHEN EVALUATING COMPETING PROPOSALS IN B2B
61%	HUMAN INSIGHTS MUST PRECEDE HARD ANALYTICS IN B2B
62%	IN B2B, OFTEN NECESSARY TO RELY ON "GUT FEELINGS"
50%	B2B BUYERS MORE LIKELY TO BUY WHEN EMOTIONALLY ENGAGED

Table 9.1 Data on the role of emotion in
B2B decision-making

It's widely accepted that buying decisions, particularly in B2B sales, are largely rational and data-driven. This belief is so well established that most marketing and sales efforts are almost solely focused on requirements, feature and competitive comparisons, and customer criteria.

Salespeople often approach the customer's buying journey from the context of how to drive rational, data-driven customer decisions. But emotions significantly influence your buyers' decisions. The B2C statistics on the impact of emotion on consumers are even more dramatic. No matter your market, you must make the customer *feel* your value.

Features, Advantages, and Benefits: *How* to Sell into the Why

As author Michael Gerber wrote, "Demographics is the science of marketplace reality. It tells you *who* your customer is… Psychographics is the science of perceived marketplace reality. It tells you *why* your customer buys."

No one in the history of humankind has ever earned a price premium from a feature dump. It's not the product or service you sell; it's why your customers buy. The *why* is the space of price premium. Sell into the why.

When teaching concepts from this chapter to sales teams, we prescribe this tangible process to put the concepts into real-world selling conversations: move from *features* through *advantages* to *benefits*, resulting in a sales tool we call the F-A-B Matrix.

Identify *Features*: Begin by listing all the features of your product or service. These are the characteristics or functionalities that it offers.

Determine *Advantages*: For each feature, consider how it provides an advantage to the customer. What does the feature enable or improve upon? This step involves understanding how the feature directly helps the customer.

Translate into *Benefits*: Finally, translate these advantages into customer-centric benefits. Think about the positive outcomes or solutions that the customer gains from each advantage *from the customer's perspective*.

Some real-world examples of products and services can be found in Table 9.2. The feature lists for these products and services are complex, detailed, and difficult to understand for anyone without specific knowledge of the features. The advantages are in everyday language. But the benefits sizzle.

Product or Service	Features	Advantages	Benefits to Customer
Camera	20 MP, 28-224mm f/3.2-6.9 Lens, 2.7" LCD Screen, 3fps Max Shooting Speed	Professional-Grade Photography and Detailed Images	Crisp, Perfect Selfies
Phone Power Bank	2000 mAh Capacity, 5V USB Port with 2.4 Amp Output	Fast Charging for Multiple Devices Simultaneously, Portable Power Source	Never Run Out of Battery on the Go
Mattress	Advanced Memory Foam, HD Coil, Moisture Wicking Tech, Mid-Loft Cover	Enhanced Support and Comfort, Temperature Regulation	Peaceful, Soothing Night's Sleep
Computer	16 GB RAM, 15" Display, Intel Core i7, 512 GB Solid State Hard Drive	High-Performance Computing Capabilities	Work and Play at Lightning Speed
Accounting Services	Reliable, Accurate Tax Returns, including Schedules A, C, and K-1	Tax Compliance, Minimized Risk of Errors	Peace of Mind, No Audits

Table 9.2 The F-A-B Matrix

How can you use this information? Share it with customers with a straightforward formula:

<Our feature> provides <advantage>,
and what that means to you is <benefit>.

Here is an example based on a variant of this formula:

OUR ELECTRONIC LOCK IS BIOMETRIC,
(FEATURE)

PROVIDING KEYLESS ACCESS.
(ADVANTAGE)

NEVER WORRY ABOUT LOSING YOUR KEYS AGAIN.
(BENEFIT)

Elaborate on and expand the simple, single-sentence version of the F-A-B as needed, depending on the scale, complexity, and scope of the offering and the deal. Utilizing F-A-B effectively can significantly enhance your sales messaging and serve as a powerful tool in closing deals.

F-A-B Exercise

The Feature-Advantage-Benefit (F-A-B) Matrix is a worksheet to help you translate the features of your products and services to meaningful, specific customer benefits.

1. Pinpoint the *specific* customer for whom you're preparing the F-A-B, possibly a customer with whom you have an upcoming sales meeting. (This approach is most effective when tailored to a specific customer and their needs rather than a generalized one-size-fits-all route.)

2. List the features, outlining the specifics of your product or service.

3. Identify advantages, showing how each feature directly impacts the customer's experience or problem-solving capability.

4. Emphasize the benefits in order to connect emotionally with the customer, illustrating how your offering meets their needs or fulfills their desires.

Be as specific, quantitative, and comprehensive as possible when completing the Feature-Advantage-Benefit Matrix.

WORKSHEET | FEATURE-ADVANTAGE-BENEFIT

FEATURE	ADVANTAGE	BENEFIT

Here's an example of the worksheet completed by one of our clients, a distributor in the horticultural industry:

WORKSHEET | FEATURE-ADVANTAGE-BENEFIT

FEATURE	ADVANTAGE	BENEFIT
Wide Range of Supplies: One-stop-shop, consolidating orders and reducing the hassle of dealing with multiple vendors.	Simplifies purchasing, allowing customers to focus on their core business operations by saving time and effort.	Reduces complexity and boosts productivity, leading to **relief** from admin burdens and **more time** for growth initiatives.
Same-Day Delivery for Local Orders: Quick access to needed supplies, ensuring timely delivery.	Prevents costly delays & downtime, enabling customers to stay on schedule and maintain service quality.	Provides **confidence** in meeting deadlines for **peace of mind** from avoiding unexpected interruptions.
Dedicated Account Managers: Personalized service with a single point of contact.	Facilitates faster problem resolution and offers tailored advice, directly addressing unique customer needs.	**Reduces frustration**, knowing they have a reliable partner who understands their challenges.
Specialized Organic and Sustainable Products: Meets the growing demand for eco-friendly products in the market.	Enhances the market positioning by appealing to environmentally conscious consumers and differentiating from competitors.	Aligns with values and enhances brand appeal, fostering **pride** in supporting sustainability and attracting new customers.
Exclusive Partnership with Leading Brands: Access to high-quality, trusted products not available elsewhere.	Ensures consistent quality to improve customer's market position and reducing risks associated with inferior products.	Provides a sense of **security and assurance** in delivering top-tier products, reinforcing their reputation for quality.
Regular Industry Updates and Training Sessions: Keeps customers informed of trends and best practices.	Empowers customers with insights to drive innovation and informed decisions, staying ahead of competitors.	Enhances customer **confidence** and positions them as proactive leaders in the industry.

Download a fillable PDF of the Feature - Advantage - Benefit Worksheet here:

Key Takeaways

- Feature selling emphasizes the attributes of a product or service, while value selling focuses on how it addresses the customer's needs. This requires a shift in perspective from a seller-centric approach to a customer-centric approach. Translate product and service features into tangible benefits that resonate with the customer's objectives.

- Connecting emotionally with customers by addressing their concerns, fears, and desires can differentiate offerings and influence purchasing decisions.

- Both positive and negative emotions play a significant role in influencing buying decisions.

- Salespeople should articulate the unique value proposition of their offerings in terms of solving customer problems, mitigating risks, and achieving desired outcomes. By articulating product or service benefits in the context of the customer's challenges or goals, salespeople can differentiate their offerings and command higher prices. The Feature-Advantage-Benefit (F-A-B) Matrix is a useful tool for this.

Keynote Audience Member Spotlight:
Marnie Ochs-Raleigh, Evolve Systems

Raising prices is about more than increasing your bottom line. It can transform how you do business and your relationship with your customers. But it can also have an enormous impact on company morale.

After a rebranding at her company, digital marketing agency Evolve Systems, CEO Marnie Ochs-Raleigh knew they needed to raise their prices. The team had elevated many of their services and were targeting bigger clients who expected more work to be done. Evolve had not fully adjusted their pricing to be aligned with this type of work, but Ochs-Raleigh knew their clients were expecting to pay more.

What she didn't anticipate was how raising prices would translate into a happier team.

"We started with our base pricing," Ochs-Raleigh says. After hearing Casey's keynote at a conference, she felt her team had to go further with pricing. "It was one of those situations where you look at the skill set of your team members, you look at what they're delivering, and you continue to get better and better when you're following your core values. This particular session just really struck close to home."

The team decided to raise prices on their services and restructure their business to focus on existing and prospective higher profit-margin clients—their A and B clients—and remove their smaller, less profitable C clients from the equation.

"Our business grew by 22 percent," she says. "But we didn't just raise our prices by 22 percent." They looked closely at what their competitive advantage was and the things they should stop doing. "Then, we identified clients that we really shouldn't work with, that will take more of our energy rather than motivate and inspire us to do better work for the clients that truly appreciate it."

This intentional shift—from focusing on quantity of work to quality of work—resulted in the team feeling more valued and invested. "Instead of begging for work, [they're saying to clients,] 'Here's what this costs and this is what we deliver,'" and being comfortable with clients walking away.

This new focus "gave us a really great stake in the ground to be able to say, 'We'll take a C client if we're needing transitional work, or if we know that it's going to be an open door into something bigger and better.' But otherwise, we no longer take a C client just to take it."

It wasn't only profitability that grew with these changes at Evolve; the company's culture improved as well. "The more you charge, the more you learn about where to put your resources." And when you charge the right price for what you provide, "you have flexibility within your business to be doing a more intentional job on your culture... When you have a good culture—when culture is working, people want to perform; it's more of a mutual respect for each other. I've learned that when I have a little extra money to be able to express gratitude in ways that match my team members' love languages, that's more impactful, and they are much more appreciative and willing to work hard."

CHAPTER 10

SOLVE A PROBLEM

Learning Objectives

1. Understand the strategy employed by Hyundai to overcome challenges in the wake of the 2008 financial crisis.

2. Explore the concept of eliminating obstacles to customer purchase to reduce price sensitivity.

3. Learn how to identify and address customer needs that you can solve unrelated to your products and services.

In 2009, following the financial crash of 2008, car manufacturers struggled to sell new cars. Remember what the economy was like then? There are many choice words to describe that time, but we'll go with *awful*. How one company successfully navigated those difficult economic conditions is the subject of our first case study.

At that time, new car sales were in the toilet. Car manufacturers were trying all kinds of things to turn that trajectory around, like giving massive discounts and rebates, but it made little difference. Even with huge promotions and incentives, people still weren't buying.

One car manufacturer did something different. Hyundai made an offer to potential customers: if they lost their job in the twelve months following their purchase of one of its cars, Hyundai would take the car back with no further payments and no impact to credit.

Hyundai grew because they solved the real problem.

This incentive was a massive coup for Hyundai. Cars flew off the lots. Hyundai grew nearly 35 percent in 2009–10, and they were one of the only car manufacturers to grow at all in 2009. They stole share from their competitors, they experienced double-digit growth even as the pie shrank, and they did it *without discounts or rebates.*

In the biggest recession in modern history, in an intensely competitive and commoditized industry, at a *massive* price premium, Hyundai achieved the highest growth rate in the automotive industry *by far.* And they grew because *they solved the real problem.* All the other car companies were throwing price at a problem that had nothing to do with price. That was not why people weren't buying.

It wasn't price stopping people; it was risk and fear.

Imagine it's 2009. You have a good job, you need a car, and you can afford a car, but you think, "I don't know, my sister-in-law just lost her job; my neighbor just lost his job. I think I'll put some new tires on the old girl and make it work a little bit longer." And then, Hyundai comes along and solves the real problem: your fear. Your fear that if you lose your job, you won't be able to make your car payments, the car will get repossessed, and your credit will be ruined. Hyundai handles that fear.

Hyundai completely removed the biggest obstacle for purchase from consumers' minds.

How can you be the Hyundai of your industry?

How can you solve a problem for customers so completely, so creatively, so uniquely, so differently that they say, "I'm going to buy from them. They're a little more expensive, but they help me do *X*."

I don't know what *X* is for your company because it depends on who your customer is—a consumer, a business, a government agency, a nonprofit—and what winning looks like for them.

To be clear, I'm not talking about the problem your core product or service already solves—how it helps customers win. Instead, I'm talking about what you can *wrap around* that product or service to solve a customer problem they would never look to your company to solve.

Although there are many ways you can help your customers win outside your core offering, your customers don't know to ask you for it. No one went to Hyundai and said, "If you offer to take my car back if I lose my job, I'll buy a car from you!" A surefire way customers want you to help them win is to give them your products and services cheaper.

Because customers don't come looking for this disruptive idea that can wrap around your offering, your salespeople have to be creative, listen, and know what the customer doesn't know. Your sales team has to crack the code of the customers' needs, wants, and pain points—because your customers cannot imagine you solving their problem for them in any other way than giving them what you already give them.

Your salespeople need to peer into your customer's world and ask themselves:

- What problems keep them up at night that I could help with?
- What pain points are they experiencing that I could ease?
- What goals do they have for their business that I could contribute to?
- What risks or obstacles prevent them from considering a purchase that I could solve?

It's important to remember two things:

1. **You can address a need for your customers that they either don't know they have or can't imagine someone in your industry solving for them.** Your product or service already solves a problem for your customers; what can you *wrap around* your core offering to solve that problem for them?

2. **Your customers aren't going to ask you for what they need.** They're not going to ask because it doesn't occur to them that you can solve any problems outside those solved by your products and services. But if you explore and uncover what problem your customers need to solve, what obstacles for purchase you can remove, or what goals they have for their businesses, and you deliver on *that* solution, you will be the stickiest partner, the only logical partner, even at a price premium.

Be the Hyundai of your industry.

Key Takeaways

- Solving a unique problem for customers can differentiate a company from competitors and drive customer loyalty, even at a premium price.
- Proactively identifying and addressing customers' unspoken needs and fears helps you provide value beyond the core product or service.
- Customers may not explicitly ask for solutions to certain problems, requiring you to actively uncover hidden pain points.
- By addressing unmet customer needs and providing solutions beyond the core offering, companies can become indispensable partners to their customers.

Client Spotlight: Alec Broadfoot, VisionSpark

Just because your competitor has lower prices doesn't mean your prices are too high.

Lack of confidence in your pricing strategy and value proposition may lead you to second-guess your prices when a competitor's are lower. This was the case for CEO Alec Broadfoot of VisionSpark, a boutique executive search firm based in Columbus, Ohio.

After more than a decade in the recruiting market, VisionSpark suddenly faced an aggressive competitor with much lower prices. "I thought we had a price issue," Broadfoot recalls. He started to question VisionSpark's pricing strategy while trying to maintain its quality standards.

After consulting with Boost, Broadfoot realized that the answer wasn't to lower prices. It was to reinforce for VisionSpark's clients why they were the better choice. They did this in four ways by

1. removing risk for clients by offering a guarantee;
2. doubling down on flat-fee pricing model and emphasizing the value to clients;
3. creating a one-pager outlining their value and expertise; and
4. offering targeted discounts to repeat clients and strategic partner referrals.

They accomplished the first step—removing risk—with a two-part guarantee. "The first component is the placement: if we don't find you someone, and you paid us a fee, we'll refund that money. And the second part of the guarantee is that if they do not work out within a certain time period, usually a year or nine months, depending on the service they choose, we will redo the search at no charge."

This guarantee, along with transparent, flat-fee pricing and clear sales messaging, set them apart from the competition and led to improved client satisfaction, resulting in repeat business and referrals. VisionSpark took steps to reduce the risk of price-related client churn by offering select discounts to those who continued to use their services or were referred by their strategic partners.

Through this process of reinforcing their value proposition with clients, the VisionSpark team realized they were often more sensitive about pricing than their clients were, underestimating what clients would pay for valuable services. Salespeople grew to understand that the right clients are willing to pay more for quality and value.

The confidence that emerged from this shift empowered the sales team at VisionSpark to defend pricing and effectively articulate the firm's value. And it has paid off: the company now charges several times more than when it started twelve years ago. VisionSpark was able to improve its competitive position and profitability while maintaining its high standards of service.

"When you have competitors who are willing to do the work for pennies, you have to remind yourself that they're not doing the job that you can do," Broadfoot says. "You're sticking to your guns about the value that you provide."

CHAPTER 11

DON'T SIGNAL LOW QUALITY

Learning Objectives

1. Explore the concept of the Price-Quality Effect and its implications for pricing strategy.
2. Understand how pricing signals can influence customer perceptions of quality.
3. Learn the importance of conveying a signal of high quality with pricing to differentiate from competitors.

You can send a signal of high quality—or low quality—with your pricing. This is called the Price-Quality Effect, in which we infer quality from pricing: If it's expensive, it must be good. If it's cheap, it must be bad. It goes along with the classic refrain, "You get what you pay for." It's why you would never eat at an all-you-can-eat 99¢ shrimp buffet.

My second case study, a story from my personal life, illustrates this effect. Over the years, I have done volunteer work in Africa, and some years ago, I decided I wanted to stay after my volunteer commitment and do something that had been on my bucket list: a photography trek with mountain gorillas.

I contacted several companies who could help me arrange the required permits and organize all the logistics of the trek, told them how long I wanted to stay, the type of accommodations I wanted, and so forth, and asked for quotes.

I received five quotes, and within a few minutes of reviewing the pile, I could see that every single quote's itineraries and descriptions were almost exactly the same. As in, nearly word for word. The same description of the majestic creatures I would enjoy in the heart of Africa, the same description of the delicious food, the gorgeous views, and the well-appointed lodgings. The quotes were virtually identical in every way, including pricing. Except for one: Kori Safaris. This company's price was *far* below what the other companies quoted. In fact, it was about half the price of the others. What do you think my reaction was?

What's wrong with this tour?

Why was the price so low? Was I gorilla bait? Would I be hunting my own food? Would I *be* the food? Would I be sleeping with the gorillas? Or was it a bunch of guys in monkey suits? Why was this tour so cheap compared to all the others?

I can assure you that the price tag alone was what had me asking these questions. The quote document looked like all the other quote documents, the website looked like all the other websites, and the list of included amenities and features looked like all the other lists. It was just the price tag, but that was enough. Kori was out.

We can send a signal of high *or low* quality with our pricing. The Price-Quality Effect is real. What kind of signal do you want to send?

You know from being a consumer yourself that there is such a thing as suspiciously cheap, and there is such a thing as *reassuringly expensive*. I would wager that there are times when you have put the more expensive version of something in your cart because you want high quality. You may have had no other data to support that you were getting the better version, but you used price as a proxy for quality.

There are industries where this effect matters a lot—where customers use price as a primary indicator of quality—and other industries where it plays a much smaller role in customers' estimation of quality. But there is no industry in the world where this effect doesn't matter at all. The implication for your salespeople is that some of your customers, some of the time, on some of your products or services, on some of your opportunities, are judging your quality based on your price. What are your prices telling them about you?

> There is such a thing as suspiciously cheap, and there is such a thing as reassuringly expensive.

But What About the Law of Demand?

As anyone who's ever taken an economics class knows, the Law of Demand states that a higher price leads to a lower quantity sold and that a lower price leads to a higher quantity sold. Business leaders' and salespeople's real-world experience substantiates this law. Nonetheless, it's wrong at least some of the time. In Chapter 3 ("Lies We Learned in Economics Class), I already shared some of the reasons this "law" is more of a general guideline.

The CEO of a successful manufacturing company once asked me what drives exceptions to the Law of Demand. In his own company, he had seen a dramatic and unexpected *increase* in sales volume when they raised the price of one of their product lines.

How can volume increase with price? As counterintuitive as it may seem, higher prices can lead to higher sales volume because those higher prices signal superior quality, especially in those industries where other direct and tangible quality and value comparisons are difficult.

Customers pursuing a certain level of quality start to focus on your solution, which they had dismissed previously. In other words, you may attract a different category of customers who seek a different caliber of product or service. I know a consultant who doubled his prices to try to manage demand, as he was at capacity. What happened? Demand for his services rose by 20 percent. He was now seen as a different caliber of expert in the space and taken more seriously by larger firms with bigger budgets. (He was still working a ton, but now he was making boatloads more money.)

Charging an appropriate price premium for value sends the message that you offer a superior product or service. Don't be suspiciously cheap!

Key Takeaways

- Pricing can serve as a powerful signal of quality, influencing customer perceptions of value and credibility.
- Suspiciously low prices can evoke doubts about product quality and credibility, leading customers to question the value proposition.
- Reassuringly higher prices can convey a signal of premium quality and attract higher-caliber customers seeking superior products or services.
- Customers use price as a proxy for quality to some degree in every industry, although the magnitude may vary depending on customer preferences and market dynamics.

Client Spotlight:
Reid Hutchison, H-O-H Water Technology

For salespeople focused on winning new clients, the instinct to discount can be strong. In times of growth, when the emphasis is on bringing in new business, reducing price can seem like the easiest way to get prospective clients on board.

When you discount, you may be setting yourself up for a mixed bag of clients—not to mention making your company's growth less sustainable from a financial perspective.

Reid Hutchison, the COO of water technology company H-O-H, anticipated these challenges during a recent period of growth. He knew that his sales team needed the confidence to pursue aggressive growth *without* leaving money on the table.

"I already understood how powerful pricing was as a lever for our profitability," he says. "I already knew we were making progress at adding volume growth and getting our sales team focused on growing. But I knew I did not have a solution yet for growing more profitably, more efficiently." Salespeople were discounting—and pre-discounting—out of fear of losing business. Hutchison wanted to focus on building confidence and negotiating stronger price increases.

H-O-H is a seasonal business, and this was at the start of the busy spring season. Business was starting to pick up. The sales team worried that now wasn't the time to turn their attention toward training for pricing decisions. But Hutchison knew the sooner they did the training and implemented what they learned, the sooner they'd see improvement.

"My issue was: how do I teach my team this? I have books on pricing. I've studied. I've been running my business for a few years, and even I am working to tie these concepts together. I know the pressure when you're in the room with the client negotiating and wanting the business," he recalls. "How am I going to help them get this concept? Because it's one part math and one part psychology."

Boost's program clarified for the sales team how powerful pricing is as a lever for profitability. And it had a positive impact on the company's margins.

"A significant part of our story this year is that our gross margins are about 2 percent higher than they were this time last year. And our revenues have grown," he says. "Some of that is definitely that our cost of goods came down, but we know that a good portion as well is us negotiating stronger and stronger price increases. It really has cemented, at least for a majority of folks, that, wow, this is a powerful lever."

The mindset shift among the team—and not just salespeople, but also operations and leadership, who participated in the training as well—has been palpable. Hutchison illustrates this with a story: "We had a large healthcare system that was putting their business out to bid. Maybe between $100,000 and $200,000 of business, a competitive RFP. And we knew we were raising our prices significantly because we were not making enough money for what we were serving. Directly from our training was alignment among the sales team involved that it was not worth keeping this business at our current price. It was hurting us more than helping us. And that's usually an incredibly hard, uphill battle; usually, the team is already prediscounting, and they're afraid of losing the business."

Instead of adjusting their number down when the client told the sales team they needed to sharpen their pencils, the team thought, *Actually, this is good news. That's a love letter. They want to do business with us.*

"To have a team that was not prediscounting, that was comfortable walking away from the business unless we could price increase—I was overjoyed," Hutchison says. And that confidence among the team paid off. "What we expected would happen happened, which is that they came back to us. We earn maybe an additional $50,000 of gross profit a year, based on the price increase, which makes it actually worth doing business with them. And we beat out some large significant competitors that have technically more capabilities than us. But we are generally the better partner because we have enough capability, but we are small enough to serve and care."

As a third-generation business owner, Hutchison recognizes the importance of training for pricing decisions and the impact it can have on the growth and success of his business. "To really graduate and mature to a higher level—you don't do that unless you've got a command of the pricing discipline." There's no way to finance growth, he says, without figuring out pricing first.

Going forward, pricing training will be a prerequisite for anyone in sales and anyone in a senior role for service. Making pricing a discipline is now "a core part of our organization's culture."

CHAPTER 12

PRICE OBJECTION HOW-TO

Learning Objectives

1. Discover how to defend the unique value proposition of your products or services.
2. Learn an effective formula for responding to price objections with confidence.
3. Understand the role of questions in price-objection handling.

One of our clients is a distributor of replacement parts for commercial kitchens in South Texas. This distributor, whom I'll call Quality Kitchen Parts, has by far the best geographic footprint, the best inventory, and the most trained sales and service staff in the industry in their region.

In other words, if you have a restaurant in South Texas and anything breaks, these are the people you want.

This company is the best at what they do, but they were underpricing themselves because of a common customer tactic: the price-match request.

Here's an example:

A business owner walks into one of Quality's distribution centers on a Saturday morning and says, "Hi! I'm Hot Mama from Hot Mama's Rib Joint. My fryer's down, and I need this part. Do you have it?" She shows her phone to the person working the counter—a photo and part name from a link to buy the product from an online store:

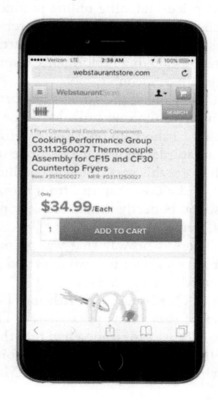

The Quality counter person says, "I believe we do, Hot Mama. Let me just double-check... Looks like we have six. How many do you need?"

Hot Mama: "Oh, just the one, thanks."

Counterperson: "Alright, I'll go grab it."

Hot Mama stops her: "Hang on a second, how much does it cost?"

Counterperson: "It's $40.16."

"Well," Hot Mama says, "I can get the same thing online for $34.99!"

And what does Quality do? *They match the online price.*

When I heard this story during a training program, I found out that price-matching online products was their policy. I asked them why they price matched. "It's the same part!" I said, "No, it's not the same part!" They said, "Yes—both are the Cooking Performance Group C15-C30 countertop fryer thermocouple."

I said, "No, they aren't the same! The part she can get online is sitting two days away in Idaho or who knows where. It's going to show up on Tuesday. Hot Mama got in her car on a Saturday morning and drove to you before the lunch rush to get this part. You will go nine feet behind you to grab it, and eleven minutes from now, she's frying up Tater Tots. You honestly think she's leaving without it for a price difference of $5.17?"

No. Way. There is no way that was going to happen. The hassle of a fryer down for two days and possible lost revenue isn't worth saving $5.17.

The team at Quality argued with me. They said she would have left if they didn't price match. They believed this to be true because Hot Mama had told them so. She'd said, "If you don't match this price, I'm going to buy it online." But what was really going on? Hot Mama *projected a volume threat* where one didn't exist. (In Chapter 2, we talked about customers projecting phantom volume threats to get discounts.) I don't blame Hot Mama for doing that— she was just trying to see what she could get away with.

The underpricing opportunity at Quality is probably perfectly obvious to you. But are your salespeople guilty of the same thing? Are they doing unnecessary and fear-based discounting? It's easy to diagnose this pernicious behavior in other companies, but sometimes, we're too close and can't see when we're doing it ourselves.

Quality thought the two parts—their part, in stock and on hand, and the other part, stored a thousand miles away in some warehouse—were the same. But Hot Mama could walk out the door with her part that day if she bought from Quality, and that was worth a different economic value to her.

Other potential costs factor into the online part. Maybe there was a cost to ship the part (that might have wiped out the $5.17 then and there). Or maybe when the part arrived on Tuesday, it was the wrong part, or it was the right part but was damaged. That's more pain and frustration for Hot Mama. Think of return policies, restocking fees, and warranties. The list keeps growing. The only thing the online part came with was... *nothing else.*

I asked the team, "Do you know what *your part* comes with?" Forty knowledgeable sales and service staff with a combined 390 years of experience stared back at me. "Your part comes with all of you. You've been in Hot Mama's restaurant seven times in the past four years. You can walk straight to her fryer, install it, and service it. You can back up the warranty that you offer that the online company doesn't. Do you know what you're selling yourselves for when you match your price to that? *Absolutely nothing.*"

Hot Mama came to Quality because Quality's part came with their sales and service staff and all that came with those valuable resources.

Let me take this opportunity to strike a bad word from your vocabulary: commodity. Like Quality Kitchen Parts, what you sell is not a commodity. Unless you can open a newspaper today and look up the price per pound of what you sell, you don't sell a true commodity. Unless the very best and the very worst in your industry sell for the exact same price, you do not sell a true commodity. (Otherwise, the company with the lowest price would have all the market share.) There are very few true commodities in this world. If you're holding this book, it's highly unlikely you sell one of those few products. Thinking that what you sell is simply a commodity is killing your profitability.

I asked Quality's salespeople to make a list of all the things that were different and special and valuable about customers buying from them versus buying online. Together, they came up with a top 25 list. They printed it on cards that they put in all their distribution centers.

Thinking that what you sell is simply a commodity is killing your profitability.

Now, when a customer comes in and says, "I can get the same thing online for cheaper," the person behind the counter hands her one of these cards and says, "We know you have a choice. We know there are other places to buy these products. However, we believe we offer substantial value over buying online. Here are the top 25 reasons we believe this to be true. My personal favorite is number 6."

You can take away two things from this story and apply to your business.

First, your customers will tell you they can get your products elsewhere for cheaper. It doesn't matter if you are in an extremely competitive, commoditized space where you sell the same thing as somebody else or in an extremely differentiated end of the industry. *Your customers will say this to you because they are humans.* It doesn't mean your prices are too high. It means they don't want to part with their resources.

> If your salespeople are unprepared for price objections, there will be one of two outcomes: they will discount, or they will lose the sale.

Second, and the more important takeaway from this story, is that your salespeople must be prepared for your customers' price objections. If your salespeople are unprepared for price objections, there will be one of two outcomes: they will discount, or they will lose the sale.

How to Prepare for Price Objections and Confidently Defend Price

The starting point for achieving higher prices and defending prices is always value. You must have a solid product or service. If you don't, pricing is not your problem. Fix your quality first.

But if you have a high-value offering, how do you defend pricing against a barrage of objections from customers, which arise in spite of your compelling value proposition? How do you hold the line in the face of constant feedback from customers that your prices are too high? (Remember that customer feedback is polluted with self-interest, and it cannot be mistaken for market intel.) The answer is a simple equation:

$$\text{Messaging} + \text{Preparation} = \text{Confidence}$$

Let's start with **messaging**. When customers object to your price, how do your salespeople respond? They must know what message to deliver for each question or objection they hear about price. For example:

"I can get this product cheaper elsewhere."

"I have three other quotes. If you can match their price, I'll go with you."

"None of your competitors are increasing prices right now."

"This price is outside our budget."

"I'm not willing to absorb your cost increases from inflation."

Your salespeople must be prepared to respond confidently and effectively to the price objections they most commonly hear. It's not as if there are one hundred different objections; you hear the same ones over and over, and the objections boil down to a handful of flavors.

Let's imagine your people tend to deal with the same five core price objections. Pull together the people at your organization who are most skilled at creating value messages to prepare responses to those objections. (If you have 20 different people selling your products or services, you don't want each one coming up with their own responses to the five objections—that's one hundred different independently derived messages. You don't want that many different value messages floating around in your marketplace!)

So, I Need a List?

For Quality, there were two parts to the message: first, the printed card with the Top 25 list and second, the counter person's verbal message accompanying the card.

Don't get hung up on the printed list. In most selling situations, there's no place for a tool like that. As you know, most price objections aren't answered with a printed piece of material or even a digital version but, instead, on the spot by the salesperson responding to the customer.

As such, I want to clarify: the purpose of the Quality story is to ensure that the *message itself* is well developed.

Quality Kitchen Parts printed their messaging on an actual card because the person delivering the message was not a salesperson. The person behind the counter when a customer entered the distribution center was a warehouse manager. Unlike trained sales professionals, Quality's warehouse managers weren't particularly comfortable with confrontational price discussions. So, the card served as a shield she could hide behind that gave her confidence.

In this way, a prepared piece can be quite helpful, especially for non-salespeople in your organization who might face price objections but may lack the personality traits or training of someone well-equipped to deal with confrontation. This might include people in customer service, installation, field teams, and so on.

> If your team wouldn't benefit from such a prepared marketing piece, given the nature of how price objections are fielded at your company, skip it. Remember, the key isn't the *medium* but the *message itself.* Don't ever skip preparing the message!

A key learning from the Hot Mama story is this: the right time to formulate objection response messaging is not the moment the customer throws an objection at you. Create this messaging in advance.

I recommend creating a price objection response document for internal use, what I call a Price Objection FAQ, which lists the talking points, questions, and facts that are most convincing when customers say, "Your price is too high." List the top price objections your salespeople hear frequently and the best value-based responses for each of those objections. Then, distribute that document to your sales team. This is a particularly helpful document to have during a price increase, but it's important to have your messaging in place for every sale, no matter what's happening with pricing.

This document needn't be a verbatim script. A bulleted list of key talking points works even better, allowing each salesperson to put the content into their own words and style.

The key to mastering price objections lies in understanding the value of your offering and effectively communicating that value to your customers. Your sales team must be armed with the right messaging to confidently address common objections. It's not enough to react on the fly. By proactively creating a Price Objection FAQ, you equip your team with a structured framework for responding to objections with value-based answers. This valuable resource ensures consistency and effectiveness in handling objections.

Sometimes, when I dive into data with sales teams, and I see a discounted deal, I'll ask why they discounted. They reply, "We felt like we had to give them something."

"I had to give them something" is code for "I didn't have a better answer ready." Have a better answer ready. Because customers *will* ask.

How many dollars and hours has your company poured into price objection messaging? For most companies, the answer is exactly zero. It's likely that your organization has spent a significant amount of time and money on other kinds of messaging: website, marketing collateral, trade association booths, and advertising. You've invested in value messaging, and you *hope* your people can successfully rearrange that sales messaging on the fly to defend prices. Some of your people probably can. Some may struggle.

> "I had to give them something" is code for "I didn't have a better answer ready." Have a better answer ready. Because customers *will* ask.

Investing in messaging—crafting compelling objection responses just as you invest in articulating your value proposition—is the first step in helping your team be more adept at defending prices with conviction. As a reminder, here's the full formula:

$$Messaging + Preparation = Confidence$$

While messaging lays the foundation for addressing price objections, it is through *preparation* that this foundation is solidified. By and large, companies do a better job with messaging than with preparation. This isn't surprising because so many sales teams are doing more with less—serving customers, churning out proposals, solving problems, chasing business—that they don't have time to practice their messaging.

Don't overlook the importance of preparation because your team is caught up in the hustle of day-to-day sales activities. This is critical even for your seasoned salespeople. World-class athletes don't show up just for games; they understand the importance of regular practice to hone skills to perform at their best during the game.

It will do your organization no good if you generate the world's best Price Objection FAQ, email it to all of your salespeople, and it sits there in their inbox. They have to open up the document and speak the words—to the mirror, to their dog, to each other. Your salespeople have to internalize the messaging. They have to say it until they feel comfortable saying the words, until the responses are second nature. It needs to be in their own voice, words, and style.

I know salespeople may balk at this suggestion, but the most effective way to practice price objection responses is by role-playing. Have your sales teams divide into groups and take turns playing the customer objecting to price and the salesperson responding to price objections. This is not about memorizing your messaging; it's about ensuring your salespeople internalize the message to hone their ability to handle the objections and questions they receive with fluency and ease.

Preparation involves more than just familiarizing oneself with the content of the messaging; it entails active engagement, practice, and refinement. By engaging in preparation, salespeople not only become adept at addressing objections but also develop the agility to adapt their responses to diverse customer scenarios. As such, while messaging provides the framework, preparation is the process through which this framework is reinforced and integrated into the dynamic realm of pricing interactions.

Having a solid, well-practiced message built on the value of your offering naturally leads to confidence in the sales and pricing process. It will allow your salespeople to hold the line on pricing, avoid unnecessary discounts, and earn more money.

An enormous part of successful pricing performance is confidence, and the keys to confidence are messaging and preparation. Put some elbow grease into developing answers to price objections, and then practice them until you deliver them with fluency and confidence. It's a simple formula. But it works.

> Having a solid, well-practiced message built on the value of your offering naturally leads to confidence in the sales and pricing process.

Neuroscience, Questions, and Price Objections

How do neuroscience and questions factor into handling price objections?

What if your salespeople responded to your customers' price objections with thought-provoking, authentic questions to help them reach the appropriate conclusion about the value of your solution? By asking targeted questions, they can prompt the customers' brain to consider buying at your price, which, in turn, increases the likelihood that they will.

This is possible because of a mental reflex called *instinctive elaboration*, in which the human brain reflexively seeks to answer a question.

If I ask you, for example, "What color is your shirt?"

For a moment, my question takes over your thought process, and you focus solely on your shirt, even if just for a fraction of a second. Your brain is considering the answer to my question and is physiologically incapable of thinking about anything else, at least for a split second.

How is this useful in pricing? Imagine this: The customer expresses concern about fees, budget, a competitive quote, or some other price-related objection. In this situation, too many salespeople eagerly steamroll the customer with their value proposition. Instead, ask open-ended questions designed to understand what's underneath the price objection. Seek to elevate the conversation beyond the transactional level.

If you respond to price objections with questions, the customer's brain reflexively seeks to answer your questions. The customer literally can't contemplate their price objection or anything else while the question you posed occupies their brain. What a powerful sales tool!

How else can questions help you earn higher prices? By reducing resistance.

People love to buy, but they hate to be sold to. When engaging with your salespeople, customers have their guard up. That resistance springs into action during price conversations in the form of price objections. Should sellers meet resistance with resistance? No. If a customer pushes back on price, and you push back on their objection, the result is two parties pushing against each other, akin to two immovable brick walls. Instead, leverage questions to reduce resistance. Genuine, helpful questions can move the sale forward and help the customer make a prudent choice for themselves without high-pressure pushback.

Using questions in pricing negotiations mirrors the philosophy of judo, where the art of pulling subtly redirects resistance, proving more effective than direct confrontation. Likewise, in Kung Fu, practitioners learn to flow with their opponent's energy rather than directly opposing it, achieving their goals with greater finesse and efficiency. So, too, with price objections. Like Bruce Lee said, "Be water, my friend."

Key Takeaways

- Messaging + Preparation = Confidence. Confidence in defending price stems from a combination of solid messaging, proactive preparation, and regular practice. Sales teams armed with these tools are better equipped to hold the line on pricing, avoid unnecessary discounts, and ultimately increase profitability.

- Your product or service is not a commodity; it offers unique benefits and value propositions that competitors cannot match. Highlighting these differences can justify higher prices and discourage unnecessary discounting.

- Consistent, compelling messaging is crucial for addressing price objections. Creating a framework, such as a Price Objection FAQ document, equips salespeople with the tools to handle objections confidently.

- Practice makes perfect: Role-playing and practicing objection responses are essential exercises for sales teams to internalize messaging and respond confidently in real-world scenarios. Regular practice helps salespeople develop fluency and adaptability in addressing objections.

- Asking thought-provoking questions can reduce resistance and direct customer focus toward value (over price).

Client Spotlight: Brent Darnell, John Henry Foster

It is common for salespeople to have a need for approval, which can get in the way of sales success. They're so worried about what the customer thinks of them that they may fold in the face of customer objections and price pushback. Combine this mindset limiter with sellers being too trusting about what customers share about pricing, and margins are at risk.

Brent Darnell, sales leader at John Henry Foster, sees these mindset saboteurs in his salespeople. In a company based on long-term relationships with customers, it can be hard for salespeople to recognize when prospective and existing customers aren't telling them the full truth.

John Henry Foster is an 80-year-old provider of hydraulic, pneumatic, automation, and compressed air solutions. They are 100 percent employee-owned and focused on people over products. Their 30 outside salespeople are embedded in the communities where they work across territories in Illinois, Missouri, and Kansas. "They live there, they grew up with their customers, their kids play baseball and softball together, they go to church together, they see each other at the grocery store," Darnell says. It's a powerful way to build business relationships, but it can also lead salespeople to believe prospects are telling the truth when they say their price is too high.

"We struggle with that," Darnell says. He tells his salespeople, "We're not saying your prospects are lying to you. But they're not telling you the truth, either because they don't know all the information, because they're not really the ultimate decision maker, or because they're doing the same thing you're doing—they're curating the information they give you."

One of the ways Darnell and other sales leaders have worked to combat this need for approval and lack of healthy skepticism is by talking openly about the self-limiting beliefs each person faces. Darnell says. "When I'm riding with them [on a sales call], we say, 'Okay, we're going into this call, [and we know] we have a lot of need for approval.'"

The process has led to conversations about how each member of the sales team is wired, why they make the decisions they make, and what they need to work on. "It's done in a manner that's not threatening, and it's not demeaning; it's all developmental: *How do I help you grow?*"

In addition to being prepared to have hard conversations with customers and prospects around price, the sales team also works on reframing their thinking from worrying if the customer likes them to whether or not the customer values them.

They have incorporated discussions around pricing into their monthly sales meetings. Hearing success stories from salespeople who have raised their margins gives the rest of the team a boost of confidence going into their own sales calls. A lot of that success, Darnell says, is a result of articulating the value they bring "beyond just selling you pieces and parts."

"We got better at saying, 'Yes, we have a price increase,' but reminding [customers] of the other things we do as a company that add value," he says of those sales team-wide conversations. "Everybody was on the same page about how to communicate that."

The mindset shift from being worried about the customer's approval to believing in the value you provide when you deliver what you promise has helped salespeople have more confidence in price discussions. "We've turned it into more of a positive," Darnell says. He tells salespeople, "I don't want you walking in there being a complete jerk [to a customer]. But you can't let him run over you. Realize when it kicks in: *Am I doing this because of my need for approval?*"

Darnell adds, "My argument is if the customer and I agree on a scope of work, and we agree on a price, and I deliver what I said I would," the customer should never say your prices are too high. Shifting their mindset from a focus on margins and pricing to a focus on value has helped limit the negative impact of the need for approval among salespeople, and it led to a seven-figure increase in profitability.

CHAPTER 13

COST OF FAILURE

Learning Objectives

1. Explore the concept of the cost of failure and its significance in defending price premiums.
2. Learn how (and how not) to effectively leverage the cost of failure as a sales tool to educate customers and guide them toward prudent purchasing decisions.
3. Understand how to identify, calculate, and represent quantitative and qualitative costs of failure.

Everyone has heard the phrase "You get what you pay for," and most of us have had to learn that lesson the hard way once or twice in our lives. How frustrating, how time-consuming, and how expensive is fixing a problem just because we chose an inferior solution to save a little money on the front end?

What does this mean for your business? Think about what happens if your customer buys the wrong product or buys from someone who can't do what you do. What are the negative consequences in your industry for customers who shortcut quality for price, now facing significant challenges and even failure?

We call this the cost of failure. In sales, we can use the cost of failure to create context for price premium. The goal is to articulate the cost of failure such that your price premium appears as nothing more than an affordable insurance policy against that cost of failure.

Leveraging the cost of failure sales tool involves two steps:

1. **Prepare:** Do the homework to identify and estimate the cost of failure *before* sitting with your customer. How much and in what ways could it cost your customer to buy something that isn't as effective as your solution? How much time and money will it cost them? How will it impact their customers and their brand, how much risk does it pose, and how many hassles and headaches could it cause? Prepare to share the information. What is the most effective way to share the information to ensure the customer looks beyond a cheaper competitive price to understand hidden costs? How, when, and under what circumstances will you leverage this sales tool?

2. **Introduce:** To educate the customer about their options and help them make a prudent choice, the sales team must bring the cost of failure into the conversation in a professional, diplomatic, and accurate manner.

Here's how this unfolds in the real world: the customer compares your price to your competitor's—you're 5 percent higher, $2 more per pound, or $10 more per hour—and those price premiums feel huge to the customer.

But when we stack those higher prices against the cost of failure—of going the cheap route and getting burned—those price premiums are dwarfed by the painful and significant costs of failure. If the competitor fails to deliver the new equipment on time, causing expensive downtime and idle crews, or the competitive marketing agency lacks creative and operational resources to deliver a world-class ad campaign, resulting in lackluster sales, your 5 percent more becomes a low premium to pay to avoid the costly problems incurred by a lower-quality product or service.

If your company ensures the customer never incurs the costs and problems the cheaper alternative will create, then your price premium is nothing more than an affordable insurance policy against that cost of failure. The goal is to help your prospective customer understand that so your salespeople can sell more successfully and maintain the price premium that you deserve for your value.

Initially, some of our clients expressed discomfort about the cost of failure before fully grasping our approach, worrying the concept was rooted in competitive smear campaigns or smarmy tactics to manipulate customers. All these clients are ethical, fair, with high integrity, and I assume the person holding this book shares those values. As such, I'd like to address these concerns directly.

If your company ensures the customer never incurs the costs and problems the cheaper alternative will create, then your price premium is nothing more than an affordable insurance policy against that cost of failure.

1. This advice isn't about trashing the competition. There's a *right* way to help your customer see that your firm, your products, and your services will be the safest bet and that the gap between the competitor's price and yours is a small price premium to pay to ensure excellent results. So, when a potential customer tells you they have a cheaper offer, help them see the true cost of going the cheaper, inferior route, not just in the product or service itself, but how it will impact their business and their life.

2. This advice isn't about manipulation or getting customers to do something counter to their own best interests. It is about educating the customers on the cost of failure and the negative impacts of inferior alternatives, so they can make a prudent choice for themselves and their business.

What Are the Costs?

Summarize these costs of failure comprehensively in qualitative and quantitative terms. Here are some of the ways your customer will be affected by choosing a cheaper, lower-quality solution:

Financial cost: This is the most obvious way your customer will be impacted. Highlight the direct and indirect financial impacts of choosing a cheaper, inferior path.

Time: This is frequently overlooked as a cost of going cheaper. The customer fails to account for the incremental time that workers, managers, and even their customers will have to put in with a lower-quality solution because it's less efficient and takes more steps. How is time throughout the process impacted by this choice?

Efficiency: Examine the impact of your solution on the customer's efficiency compared to that of an inferior solution. If the alternative process works slightly slower, if it slows down a manufacturing process, or if their sales process would be negatively affected, articulate that cost of failure for the customer.

Headaches: Are there tasks that will be harder or more frustrating to execute with the competitive product or service? Where would your customer experience more difficulty, frustration, slowdowns, or hassle? Less peace of mind around the alternative solution? This cost of failure can be especially powerful when the alternative solution is an internal manual process doing nothing for their business, and your solution would make their life a lot easier.

Employee engagement: Frustrating tasks can cause active employee disengagement. Would the competitor's inferior product or service make the customer's employees frustrated or make it harder for them to do their jobs? (Employee disengagement and staff turnover are both costly!)

Risks: What risks would the lower-cost/lower-quality alternative create inside and outside their organization? This could be a risk to safety, customers, or financial performance. Highlighting risk as a cost of failure can stimulate buyers' urgency.

Customer impact: If the competitor's inferior product or service does not perform to your customer's expectation, what impact does that have on their ability to serve *their* customers? If there is a service interruption, if there is downtime in their process, in their manufacturing facility, in their service operation, or in their ability to serve their customers, it could result in lost sales and profit, which can tie back to cost.

Brand impact: If the competitive solution doesn't perform as well as yours and this can negatively impact their customers, what effect does that have on their reputation? Their long-term brand image?

Dos and Don'ts of the Cost of Failure

Don't trash your competitors. Don't be unnecessarily negative or nasty about your competition.	→	**Do** professionally, diplomatically, and accurately educate the customer about their options.
Don't be vague. Unclear and nebulous claims about costs, risks, and downsides with no specifics are hard for customers to grasp and invite skepticism.	→	**Do** be as specific as possible about the impact. Quantify wherever possible. Use specific examples and stories where it's not possible to quantify. The more real you make the cost of failure for your customer, the more successful this strategy will be.
Don't exclude impact elements just because they are difficult to quantify. Don't exclude qualitative-only elements.	→	**Do** make a reasonable, educated guess at elements that are difficult to quantify. Speak to the negative impact of qualitative elements, even if neither you nor the customer can tie a specific dollar figure to the impact of those elements.

Don't make wild or unreasonable claims about the costs of failure. You will lose credibility with the customer if your claims aren't based in reality.	→	**Do** use reasonable figures. For any difficult-to-quantify elements, be realistic but somewhat conservative.
Don't communicate the costs of failure with your customer verbally only.	→	**Do** share the information visually, ideally in a graphical or pictorial way. See more on this in the shaded box on p. 215.

Don't Let Your Customers Down

Pointing out the potential costs of failure for prospects is not just a way to sell your product or service. It's about serving your customers better by protecting them from an inferior solution that won't solve their problem, and it's about protecting your deserved margins in the process. It's not about using worry and fear to manipulate your customers into buying from you. It is about educating the customers on the cost of failure and the negative impacts of inferior alternatives so that they can make a prudent choice for themselves and their business.

Don't let your customers down. If you let them purchase inferior quality at a low price, they could end up like this poor customer at a shady tattoo parlor instead of the higher priced, higher quality shop down the street:

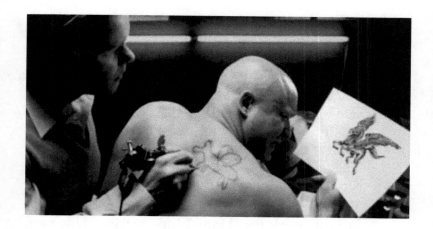

This image is from a popular internet meme that was accompanied by the phrase "You can always find someone to do it cheaper." This is true. There is no doubt that customers can find cheaper options. But it's your job to professionally and diplomatically remind them that they will get what they pay for.

In this meme, the customer wanted a Pegasus tattoo. What he got was a tattoo of a skinny hippo with wings. This plays out with your customers as well. What your customers want is Pegasus quality, but they hope to persuade you to sell it at skinny hippo pricing.

Remember, this isn't about using worry and fear to manipulate your customers into buying from you. It is about educating customers on the cost of failure and the negative impacts of inferior alternatives so that they can make a prudent choice for themselves and their business.

Let's take our skinny hippo friend, for example. When your customers say, "I have this quote from your

Customers can find a cheaper option. Your job is to remind them that they get what they pay for.

competitor; can you match the price?" and they're holding a quote for a skinny hippo with wings but want a Pegasus, how do you handle it? You have a few choices:

1. You can pass on the opportunity, knowing that your value is too high to chase that low price and low quality. You let the customer know you can't help them at that price, and they go buy the skinny hippo. That's *not* taking care of your customer; that's *not* serving their long-term needs.

2. You can match that competitor's price. You can do Pegasus work for skinny hippo pricing. However, that's *not* serving your organization's needs. You *aren't* being paid well for your value nor protecting your margins.

3. You can diplomatically and professionally educate your customer about the costs of failure, so that they can make a prudent choice for themselves and their business. This protects the customer, provides true customer service, and it protects your margins in the process.

Why Share Information *Visually* with Customers?

There are two great reasons to share your value story and the cost of failure with customers visually:

1. Different customer learning styles dictate a need for visually represented information, not only verbally communicated information. As they say, a picture is worth a thousand words. In behavioral psychology, this is called the Pictorial Superiority Effect, which is the phenomenon in which pictures are more likely to be remembered than words. (I once heard Gino Wickman, best-selling author and creator of EOS®, say that a picture is worth a thousand... dollars. I love it. Sometimes, a picture can be worth tens of thousands of dollars or more.)

2. Often, more than one decision-maker is involved in the customer's buying process. You may have a champion for your product or service *inside* the customer's organization, but that person has to convince other decision-makers that you are the right choice, especially if your product or service is more expensive. You are an expert at selling your product or service, but your customer champion is not. By providing this visual value story to that person, you extend your sales reach inside your customer's organization.

The graph below is a visual value story showing the costs of failure incurred when the customer selects an inferior competitive solution. Cost of failure elements include labor, waste, overtime, turnover related to employee dissatisfaction, and more, totaling over $225,000. In addition, other difficult-to-quantify costs of failure (lower customer satisfaction, higher risk) are included, even without specific values assigned to remind the buyer that these significant costs incurred, even if unquantifiable.

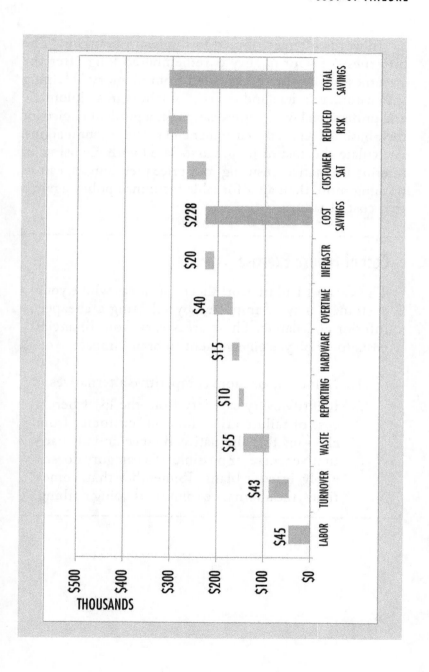

In words often attributed to Benjamin Franklin, "The bitterness of poor quality is remembered long after the sweetness of low price has faded from memory." Helping the customer understand the cost of failure in a diplomatic and professional way, so they can make a prudent choice for their business serves the customer and protects your margins. Articulate the cost of failure associated with choosing an inferior alternative, ensuring your price premium appears as nothing more than an affordable insurance policy against that cost of failure.

Cost of Failure Exercise

The Cost of Failure worksheet lists areas where your customers may be impacted by selecting a cheaper, inferior alternative. These areas vary from financial costs to employee engagement to brand impact.

1. Name one or more competitive alternatives.

2. Identify every category from the list where a cost of failure arises for your customer from choosing that alternative. Be specific and quantitative wherever possible. If a category doesn't apply, leave it blank. Remember that, sometimes, the alternative solution is doing nothing.

WORKSHEET | COST OF FAILURE

AREA OF IMPACT	COMPETITOR 1: DO NOTHING	COMPETITOR 2:	COMPETITOR 3:
FINANCIAL COSTS			
FINANCIAL COSTS (ADDITIONAL)			
TIME			
RISKS			
IMPACT TO *THEIR* CUSTOMERS			
EFFICIENCY			
HEADACHES / PEACE OF MIND			
EMPLOYEE ENGAGEMENT			
INTERRUPTIONS			

Here's an example of the worksheet completed by one of our clients, a digital marketing agency:

WORKSHEET | COST OF FAILURE

AREA OF IMPACT	COMPETITOR 1: DO NOTHING	COMPETITOR 2: LOW-COST AGENCY	COMPETITOR 3: DIY APPROACH
FINANCIAL COSTS	**Lost Opps:** No campaigns = stagnant growth. $200,000.	**Poor ROI:** Low engagement, poor-quality leads, higher acq. costs. $150,000.	**Misallocation:** Expertise gap drives poor ad spend allocation. $40,000.
FINANCIAL COSTS (ADDITIONAL)	**Share Erosion:** Lose share from lack of active engagement. $500,000.	**Rework Costs:** Redo ineffective or damaging campaigns $75,000.	**Higher Employee Costs:** Increased payroll from overtime. $425,000.
TIME	**Delay in Growth:** 12 months behind competitors in mkt recognition.	**Iteration Waste:** 150 hrs / yr on low-quality deliverables, corrections.	**Learning Curve:** 3-6 months for in-house team to learn and apply best practices.
RISKS	**Competitive:** Falling behind competitors who actively engage.	**Brand Damage:** Poor campaign quality affecting brand perception.	**Inefficiency:** Mismanaged campaigns and wasted resources.
IMPACT TO *THEIR* CUSTOMERS	**Low Engagement:** Customers unaware of new offerings.	**Negative CX:** Low-quality may frustrate prospects and customers.	**Lower Reach:** Limited internal capabilities restrict reach, customer acq.
EFFICIENCY	**Inefficiencies:** Prospects are not educated about offerings, impacting sales.	**Productivity:** Time lost with frequent fixes due to poor-quality output.	**Overburdened Employees:** Workload cuts productivity and job satisfaction.
HEADACHES / PEACE OF MIND	**Stagnation:** Growth-related anxiety from lack of marketing efforts.	**Management:** Continual back-and-forth with agency over quality issues.	**Friction:** Disagreements among team about lack of results.
EMPLOYEE ENGAGEMENT	**Low Morale:** Lack of progress impacts morale and motivation.	**Rework:** Team is disengaged from constant rework and changes.	**Burnout & Turnover:** Stress from juggling multiple roles.
INTERRUPTIONS	**Sales Pipeline:** Sales dip from lack of leads / mktg activities.	**Interruptions:** Constant changes disrupt ongoing ops.	**Op Disruptions:** In-house team diverted from core competency.

Download a fillable PDF of the Cost of Failure Worksheet here:

Key Takeaways

- The cost of failure concept emphasizes the hidden expenses and risks associated with choosing inferior products or services solely based on lower prices.
- Leveraging the cost of failure in sales involves thorough preparation to identify and estimate potential costs before engaging with customers.
- Effective communication of the cost of failure requires professionalism, diplomacy, and accuracy to educate customers about the implications of their choices.
- Sales professionals should emphasize the financial, time, efficiency, and employee engagement costs, among others, associated with opting for cheaper alternatives.
- Avoiding vague claims and providing specific examples enhances the credibility and effectiveness of the cost of failure strategy.

- The cost of failure strategy is not about disparaging competitors or manipulating customers but about serving their long-term interests and maintaining fair margins.
- Visual representation of the cost of failure can enhance customer understanding and appeal to different learning styles, facilitating buy-in from multiple decision-makers.

Client Spotlight: Andy Schuster, Matandy Steel

When you work in a commodity industry like steel processing, it can be challenging to differentiate yourself from competitors. There is a tendency to believe that you have to compete solely on price. It takes a mindset shift to realize that competing exclusively on price is unsustainable and to focus instead on the unique benefits you provide to your customers, even when these feel difficult to define.

The sales team at Matandy Steel and Metal Products, a steel service center that also manufactures metal studs and trusses, found itself in this unsustainable place. They struggled to defend pricing and faced constant pressure from customers who claimed to have better offers or market insights.

"They get beat up all the time with 'Hey, we heard [the price of steel] is going lower. Can you help us out?'" Matandy president and CEO Andy Schuster says. "Our salespeople were like, 'Well, we're just selling steel. So, we've got to be the lowest price.'"

"In our industry," Schuster says, "things don't change much... So, the price of steel we can't control."

He decided to bring in Boost to help build pricing confidence within the sales team. The first thing they did was work on mindset—shifting from a defensive stance to one of confidently defending their value proposition. Part of that training focused on being willing to walk away from unprofitable deals.

"If you have the confidence to know that what you're providing is a quality product and you're giving them value, you have to be willing to walk away if they're trying to beat you down," Schuster says. The sales team embraced the principle that not every customer is the right fit, and being willing to walk away reinforces the value of their product.

This newfound confidence extended to the management level at Matandy, enabling leaders to coach their teams effectively and reinforce Boost's pricing principles. The consistent messaging from leadership ensured that pricing became embedded in the company culture. And they continued to hammer home the message with ongoing training from Boost, transforming how they viewed and approached pricing.

"Before this, we had no tools... It was just like, 'Hey, here's the index for pricing.' But now we're looking at those indices, we're meeting a little more regularly and talking about them. Where are they going? Where do we think they're going?"

The company moved from thinking of pricing as a basic operational task to viewing it as a strategic lever. They began holding regular meetings between sales and purchasing teams to review market trends, indexes, and inventory management. This alignment helped them create a pricing strategy that supported profitability and long-term growth.

Better pricing discipline and a stronger belief in their value have resulted in measurable margin improvement, which Schuster puts at 2–5 percent. But, he says, "confidence for our sales group has been the biggest thing, and also making pricing a strategy because it wasn't really considered before."

CHAPTER 14

GIVE TO GET

Learning Objectives

1. Understand the importance of maintaining price integrity in negotiations and the consequences of offering unearned discounts.

2. Learn the concept and explore examples of "give to get" to protect margin while aligning with customer needs and preferences.

3. See how to use "give to get" to separate negotiation tactics from genuine price sensitivity and safeguard price integrity while enhancing profitability.

Besides reminding the customer of the cost of going cheaper, as shared in Chapter 13, your salespeople can employ another tactic to avoid unnecessary discounts: don't discount without changing the offering.

Imagine a scenario where DigitalEdge, a fictional digital marketing firm, has proposed a set of monthly services for a retainer of $8,000 per month. Upon reviewing the proposal, the prospective client says, "Oh, that's more than we spent with our last marketing partner. If you can do it for $6,500, we can move forward."

If the salesperson says yes, what might be going through the client's mind? Naturally, they're happy to save money, but their confidence in the salesperson's integrity might be diminished. They might wonder whether the seller would have gone lower. They may question whether the initial price was artificially inflated and the salesperson tried to get away with it. Such doubts can have significant repercussions.

When you discount prices without asking for anything in return, you are telling your customer two things:

1. **You were overpriced to begin with.** "Caving" on price in this way sends a message to your customer that there was extra margin in the deal that you were trying to sneak past them, and they caught you in the act. This quick crumble to a lower price creates suspicion and unease in your customer's mind that your pricing was set arbitrarily and unfairly high. Even if this isn't true, it's the message you send.

2. **They can continue to beat you up on price.** When you drop price without any reduction in offering, it trains your customer to keep pushing for it. They learn that all they have to do is ask you for a better price, and you will capitulate. You've done the equivalent of giving a piece of candy to a tantrum-throwing toddler to keep them quiet. They now know exactly

what button to push to get that candy next time. (Stop giving candy to crying customers!)

If you change the price and nothing about the deal changes, I call this an *unearned discount*. Unearned discounts hurt trust, and that's so important it bears repeating: unearned discounts hurt trust. (Of course, they kill profits too. But perhaps the most serious impact is lost trust with your customers.)

> When you discount prices without asking for anything in return, you are telling your customer two things: You were overpriced to begin with, and they can continue to beat you up on price.

For salespeople who believe a discount will make the customer feel good, this might feel counterintuitive. However, if you don't change something about the deal, you hurt price integrity. (I'm using *integrity* in a structural sense here, not a moral sense. Integrity rests on an exchange of value, and you've cracked it by discounting for nothing.) Maintaining price integrity is critical.

Give to Get

Instead, your salespeople must change the offering in some way in exchange for the discounted price, a so-called "give to get." Reduce scope. Reduce use of premium materials. Require a minimum order quantity. Eliminate ancillary services that are normally included with the purchase

> Salespeople must change the offering in some way in exchange for the discounted price, a so-called "give to get."

of this core product or service. Trade *something* for that price concession.

The most common "give to get" approach is descoping, but that doesn't work for every business or situation. You cannot dissect every offering without compromising the brand promise. Read through this list of options that extend well beyond traditional product or service descoping options:

Factor	"At that price, we…"
Scope	…can remodel floors 9-11 but not floor 12 as originally scoped.
Support	…can have 1 person onsite instead of 2 people.
Quality	…can use standard grade 304 but not marine-grade stainless steel 316.
Delivery Timing	…can ship it July 1 but not June 1.
Delivery Frequency	…can deliver monthly but not weekly.
Terms	…will require 50% deposit instead of the standard 25%.
Contract Length	…will need an 18-month contract instead of 12.
Service Level	…will be able to offer M-F 9-5 phone support but not 24/7.
Service Frequency	…will visit the site bimonthly instead of weekly.

Warranty	...can offer a 1-year warranty but not the standard 2-year warranty.
Returns	...must limit our return window to 14 days instead of 30 days.
Training	...can provide online training instead of in-person training.
Version	...can offer the Essentials package instead of Premium.
Refunds	...can process refunds as credits towards purchases but not cash refunds.
Customization	...can provide the standard product but not the customized version.

Besides changing the offering itself, another option is to ask for something that helps your business:

Factor	"I can make that price work if you are able to..."
Social Proof	...provide a testimonial we can use on our website.
Introductions	...make a sit-down introduction to the other VPs in your division.
Referrals	...introduce me to three potential leads in your network.
Exclusivity	...agree to exclusivity in the customer's territory.

Case Studies	...work with us on a case study about your successful use of our service.
Feedback	...meet with us after implementation to provide detailed feedback.
Data Access	...provide anonymized customer data for market analysis.
Training	...allow us to provide training for staff to maximize use of our product.

Ideally, what you give up and what the customer gives up will be equal, but if you have to give more, at least your price integrity is intact. No matter what, ask for *something*.

I'm a fan of establishing and trading options to let the customer opt into their own price sensitivity category. This helps you distinguish true price sensitivity from buying tactics. Here's an intentionally over-simplified example:

Seller: "Our chocolate cake costs $10."

Buyer: "Well, my budget is $8."

Seller: "Okay. I'd love to deliver you a chocolate cake that is delicious and still meets your budget. I can make an $8 chocolate cake that you'll love—but without sprinkles and candles."

If you say, "Okay, $8 is fine," you've hurt trust, you've cost yourself profit, and you've trained your customer to press for discounts every time forever with no penalty.

If two dollars magically appeared out of thin air, this was just a customer tactic. They were just fishing for a discount. But if they really are budget-constrained and they're perfectly fine with no sprinkles and no candles, then it's a win-win-win:

- It's a win for the buyer, who gets cake inside their budget.
- It's a win for the seller, who avoids the cost and work of sprinkles and candles.
- It's a win for trust—a win for price integrity.

(Of course, it's essential not to reduce scope to such a degree that your brand promise is compromised. Never sell your cake baked without eggs and sugar.)

If the customer really wants sprinkles and candles, they will find a way to pay the price. If they don't care very much about sprinkles and candles, they won't. Customers self-select into a price-sensitivity category based on the features they value most. This is a value conversation, not a price negotiation.

Have value conversations, not price negotiations.

Provide the customer with options, allowing them to opt into their own price-sensitivity category. Giving options around your offering

- separates negotiating tactics from true price sensitivity;
- improves your profitability; and
- protects price integrity.

Key Takeaways

- Unearned discounts erode customer trust and kill profits. Discounts without corresponding changes to the offering can signal to customers that initial prices were inflated, undermining trust and raising doubts about the seller's integrity.
- The "give to get" approach, wherein changes to the offering are exchanged for discounted prices, helps preserve price integrity.
- Offering adjustments to the scope, quality, or terms of the deal can demonstrate flexibility and responsiveness to customer needs without compromising price for value.
- While accommodating customer requests, it's crucial not to compromise on core aspects of the offering that define the brand promise.
- Changing the deal with changing price results in win-win outcomes where both parties feel they've received value, reinforcing trust and long-term collaboration.

Client Spotlight: Betsy McLarney, EMC Outdoor

Successful pricing conversations rarely start with price.

Just ask Betsy McLarney, CEO of EMC Outdoor, an out-of-home marketing agency that has been connecting buyers and suppliers of advertising for more than 25 years.

EMC acts as an intermediary, which requires the company to manage multiple pricing conversations with different partners to launch a single ad campaign.

"There's pricing psychology on both sides of the equation," McLarney says. "Our clients want [to pay] the lowest price possible, and our suppliers want [to get] the highest price."

That makes pricing *doubly* important for EMC. Their sales team has the ability to swing profitability on both sides of the equation as they negotiate distribution costs and customer pricing.

This is where seemingly small pricing details have a much larger compounding effect, McLarney points out. Salespeople were resorting to "I'll work with [this supplier] to buy this billboard; they always give me 15 percent off. I'm going to accept that without any discussion." Then, she says, the salesperson will move on, "even though we know, based on this buy, that it's not just one billboard. It's 50 billboards in 5 markets. As a result, we can apply more leverage in the negotiations with further package discounts, delivering more added value to the client."

When clients asked about price, salespeople often took the bait—focusing the conversation on price rather than value. This approach can become automatic if it goes unchecked. And it was leaving money on the table.

McLarney wanted to help her salespeople level up their pricing conversations. She brought in Boost for a ten-week course. In these sessions, the sales team dug into the concept of value and learned how to elevate value above price in all their conversations.

"If there's one thing that came out of [these] courses," McLarney says, "it's that value is greater than price. You need to be able to convey that."

In these sessions, salespeople talked about the price objections and obstacles they frequently encountered when negotiating deals. They agreed on the importance of being prepared to ask the right questions when clients tried to redirect the conversation to price and on how to use those questions effectively.

McLarney saw a transformation in her team. "It gave the team a solid level of confidence," she says.

And when the team put these Boost principles in place, there was another positive transformation: margins went up 2 percent! Considering their position in the market as an intermediary, that was a significant success.

Now, the sales team has a fresh presentation for new clients focused on how working with EMC *provides them with more value*. The benefits of working with EMC shine through and anchor the conversation around "Why you should work with us" instead of "How much you should pay us."

Through the process of focusing on value and isolating memorable value points, the team at EMC deepened their own understanding of the value they provide.

"I've found that while the work we do is valuable, the employees that provide it sometimes feel like it's not enough," says McLarney. "I say, 'No, I don't think you understand what some of the competitors are providing.' So, it's getting confident that what we have to offer is really valuable and not like what everybody else is doing."

This newfound confidence at EMC had another positive effect. Salespeople started putting items on quotes they hadn't been charging for.

They identified "wraparound fees"—international transactions, hard copy proof approvals, overnighting and rush fees—"just a whole number of [relevant] fees that, routinely, we didn't charge for." Understanding and conveying their value opened the sales team's eyes to how much they were giving away for free.

PART 5

EXECUTING ON STRATEGY

Many organizations are great at creating a strong pricing strategy, but then a disconnect arises between that strategy and its execution. In other words, what's actually happening doesn't align with the plan.

Let me take you through an example of this problem that arose with a client of ours. This company, VertiSafe Protection, manufactures fall-protection equipment: harnesses, lanyards, and all kinds of equipment that helps keep people safe when they work at heights in manufacturing, oil and gas, construction, and other environments.

VertiSafe doesn't sell directly to the end user but rather through distribution. And their pricing strategy was to sell based on volume: The bigger you are, the better price you get. The smaller you are, the less discount you get. Customers were automatically assigned discounts based on the previous year's sales volume.

Before our training with the VertiSafe sales team, the CEO told me that, with regard to these discount tiers, "we have a few exceptions, but very few. My sales VP has to approve all of those, but you're going to see a very clean data set because we're automatically assigning based on sales volume."

Here is the graph I created based on their data:

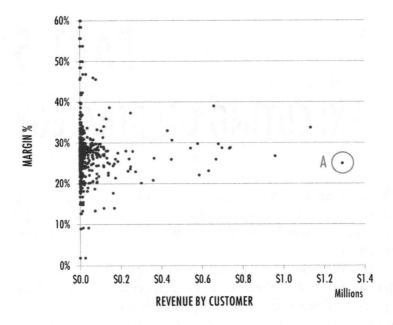

What you're looking at is a scatter plot where every data point is a customer, plotting the customer's gross margin % (y-axis) against the revenue generated by that customer's purchases. For example, Dot A is VertiSafe's biggest customer, a distributor buying $1.3 million in fall protection equipment at about 25 percent gross margin.

Now, based on what the CEO told me about automatically assigning customers to discount tiers by sales volume, I expected to see big customers buying at a deeper discount (lower margin) and smaller customers buying at a lesser discount (higher margin). But that is not what this shows or doesn't show it very cleanly. What you see is a lot of smaller customers buying at a deep discount.

So, I showed the graph to the CEO and said, "What's going on in this lower-left-hand corner?" And then, "Oh, I think you probably just graphed it wrong." (*Twenty-five years of working in Excel, a certified Six Sigma Black Belt from GE, a chemical engineer from Case Western Reserve University, and I don't know how to graph something in Excel? Really?!* I didn't say it, but I thought it.)

But the controller in the room said, "No, she didn't graph it wrong. This is the right data. This is a real effect." And the CEO said, "But I don't understand. How could this be true? I thought we automatically assigned customers based on sales volume. Why is my sales VP approving all these exceptions? Who the heck are these customers? Who's that customer?" He pointed to a dot at the bottom left.

I looked at my chart and said, "Oh, that customer is ABC Distribution." He said, "I've never even heard of ABC. Why haven't I heard of ABC?" I thought to myself, *Because, like most companies, you spend all your time thinking about and talking about your top 10 customers, your top 25 customers, or your top 100 customers, and you're never down here looking at the little ones.*

Then, he said, "Who's the sales rep for ABC?" I said, "It looks like it's Jim Smith." He said, "Jim's fired!" "Hang on a second," I said." "Talk to Jim. See what Jim has to say."

The CEO asked Jim to come in, and the CEO asked about ABC. "Why are they on column F pricing? They don't have enough sales volume for column F pricing. They should be on column P pricing." Jim said, "Oh, they came to us last year in April and asked us to partner with them with a strategic discount because there was some big sales opportunity coming in the second half." The CEO asked, "What happened in the second half?" Jim looked at his shoes as he said, "That sales volume never quite materialized. And we just haven't gone back to raise prices."

You may have had this experience before—customers making big volume promises that don't quite come through. That's what had happened to poor Jim.

The CEO started pointing to other customer dots—the one who used to buy a lot but slowed down and remained on their discount tier in the hope that they'd start buying again, the one who had a warranty claim, the one who had a costly return. Those "very few" exceptions to their strategy had multiplied.

If your data reflects the same executional challenges to strategy as VertiSafe's data, I'll offer you the same advice I gave them: this isn't the time for reprimands and head-hanging. This is an opportunity to act.

How can you start to move that body of underpriced revenue up in a way that doesn't keep you up at night, horrified that you're going to lose a ton of sales volume or you're going to go out of business tomorrow because you were too aggressive? And how do you prevent those "problem dots" in the future?

You can have a detailed, well-thought-out pricing strategy, but if you don't execute it consistently and intentionally, you're missing out on opportunities. One way to ensure that your execution matches your strategy *and minimizes business risk* is by using analytical **focusing tools** and **price guidance tools**. These help you identify where to spend the least effort and take the least risk to get the biggest return and then point you to the specific segments, customers, products, services, and opportunities where you can take action.

I've divided the following seven tools into two categories: tools to help you identify opportunities for improvement (focusing tools) and tools to help you make smart decisions for your business (price guidance tools). The tools in the first category (Chapter 15) use data from your business to show you where to focus efforts and take action for a big return. The tools in the second category (Chapter 16) are general tools that anyone can use to help them make confident decisions about price relative to volume, leading to greater success and profitability.

> You can have a detailed, well-thought-out pricing strategy, but if you don't execute it consistently and intentionally, you're missing out on opportunities.

In each chapter, I'll explain how each tool works and show how it can be applied in your business. The goal is to help you make better data-driven decisions and to give you a risk-mitigated roadmap to move your business toward greater profit.

CHAPTER 15

TOOLS TO IDENTIFY OPPORTUNITY

The following tools are what I think of as focusing tools. These exception management tools help you quickly identify areas of pricing opportunity inside your business, highlighting exceptions to the rule (or exceptions to strategy) to save you time. You can attend to those customers and deals that require action rather than sifting through reports containing every customer, product, service, and deal. The data revealed with these simple tools allows you to conserve operational resources by focusing on the few rather than the many.

These tools give you and your sales team a chance to triage performance to uncover opportunities. Which customers are underpaying? What opportunity exists to address profitability for these customers? What price and margin make sense for a customer of this size and type? Where can we apply the least effort and take the least risk for the biggest benefit?

I call this idea of least effort with least risk for the biggest results the "bullets before cannonballs" approach, a concept developed in Jim Collins' seminal business book *Great By Choice*: "First, you fire bullets (low-cost, low-risk, low-distraction experiments) to figure out what will work—calibrating your line of sight by taking small shots. Then, once you have empirical validation, you fire a cannonball (concentrating resources into a big bet) on the calibrated line of sight. Calibrated cannonballs correlate with outsized results; uncalibrated cannonballs correlate with disaster. The ability to turn small proven ideas (bullets) into huge hits (cannonballs) counts more than the sheer amount of pure innovation."

Besides taking action to directly improve customer profitability, another benefit of using focusing tools with your team is that it provides an opportunity to talk as a sales team about what's happening versus what *should* be happening based on an effective price strategy. The learning that happens in these conversations is valuable, not only for the exceptions in question, but also for the salesperson's development in strategic pricing decision-making.

Apply the "bullets before cannonballs" approach to calibrate pricing strategy and minimize risk.

In this chapter, we'll look at four tools:

1. Revenue-Margin Scatter Plot
2. Revenue-Margin Heat Map
3. Pareto Chart
4. Pareto Heat Map

I've used these tools with hundreds of clients. They are an effective way to quickly see where opportunities exist in your business to help you focus on where you should take action.

Tool 1: Revenue-Margin Scatter Plot

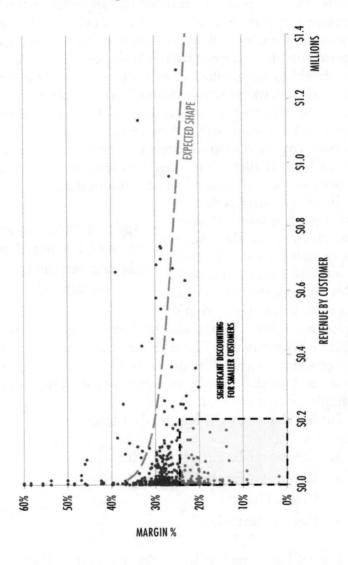

Figure 15.1 Revenue–Margin Scatter Plot

This scatter plot helps to identify the low-hanging fruit. It helps leaders and salespeople focus their efforts on areas where customers are paying too little: those customers in the lower-left-hand corner of the scatter. They are small customers generating little revenue *and* low margins, which indicates probable underpricing.

As with the VertiSafe example from the introduction to Part 5, a common pricing strategy is that bigger customers enjoy the deepest discounts and lowest prices because of economies of scale and more buying power. In such a case, I'd expect the actual data to reveal that the biggest customers enjoy the most favorable pricing, resulting in lower margins, and the smaller customers pay a higher price. What you see in the lower-left-hand corner violates that expectation, indicating a disconnect between strategy and execution.

How to Use This Tool

Looking at the exceptions in your business is a helpful focusing tool. It also saves you time. You might not be able to look at 1,000 individual data points, but you can examine 75.

One of my clients runs a weekly "Corner Club" meeting. Any sales rep with a customer in the lower-left-hand corner enters that meeting to explain why the customer is there and how they're planning to move the customer out of the corner.

The discussion certainly results in a plan for that customer, but there is also value in the discussion itself in the form of learning for the salesperson. Leaders can play devil's advocate to improve the salesperson's pricing decision-making in the future. "Sell me on why this customer should be in the lower-left-hand corner, and I'll sell you on why they shouldn't. Together, we'll make a better business decision because we've cracked this customer opportunity open and examined it from all angles. We've discussed the things that make the customer price-sensitive and the things that give us pricing power." In this process, the sales rep gets better at making decisions for tomorrow, for the next customer, for the next deal. In finding a solution for one customer, the salesperson learns how to address future customers.

Occasionally, a customer *belongs* in that corner. Maybe they're a brand-new, very large customer. They haven't bought a lot yet, but you've given them favorable pricing because you believe they're going to be tomorrow's whale. The key in this scenario is to keep an eye on that customer. They may have made big promises about what they're going to buy, but if after a month or a quarter of them not buying what they said they would, it's time to move them out of the corner by raising the price.

At a business-wide level, the scatter plot also helps leaders and salespeople see that opportunity does exist to price more consistently and effectively. Taking a 10,000-foot view of the business in this way, it's hard for a sales team to argue that they are perfect at price execution. In the face of this data, no one can dismiss price-improvement opportunities because they're only thinking of a handful of larger customers with "right" pricing.

And you can drill down and parse this data further, depending on the factors specific to your business. For example, if you sell to customers in the US and Mexico with differing price sensitivities, you might want to create separate scatter plots for each geography to see the lower-left-hand corner in each. If you operationalize this tool in your day-to-day business, you can find ways to make it specific for your company so that the data it provides is more granular and more relevant.

How often you run a revenue-margin scatter plot depends on the length of your sales cycle. You might run it once a quarter or once a month. You might even run it weekly if you have a million transactions a week, but not if you have a hundred transactions a year. Whatever the frequency, running this graph will help you identify those customers who are ripe for pricing and profit improvement.

Once you've examined the data and talked it through, raise prices thoughtfully and diplomatically to customers in that lower-left-hand corner. Understand that a small number of customers in that corner might leave with an increase, but the impact of that volume churn is low because those customers individually represent little revenue and little profit. And for the ones who stay, you will enjoy a much higher profit. Calibrate using those smaller "bullets" so you can slowly move onto larger and more profitable customers (cannon-level impact to profitability), building precision and confidence for pricing along the way.

Download the Revenue-Margin Scatter Plot Tool here:

Tool 2: Revenue-Margin Heat Map

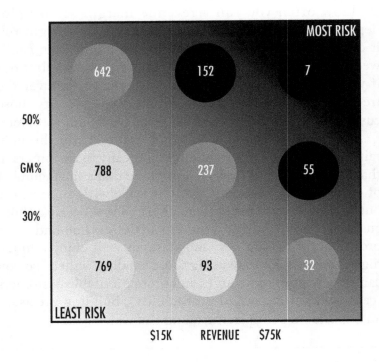

Figure 15.2 Revenue–Margin Heat Map

A full-color version of this map is available by scanning the QR code on page 249.

The Revenue-Margin Heat Map uses the same data as the Revenue-Margin Scatter Plot and is organized in a similar fashion: the upper right is where your business is making the most money, and the lower left is where you're making the least.

The benefit of the heat map, compared to the Scatter Plot, is twofold: it provides a small amount of data to take in at once (nine dots instead of the hundreds or thousands in the scatter), and it is color-coded by risk. In these ways, it can be viewed as a simplification of the scatter plot.

In the heat map shown in Figure 15.2 or by downloading the Revenue-Margin Heat Map Tool, you can see how the company's customer base is distributed according to risk:

Green = Low Risk. There is a low likelihood of losing these customers over a price increase, as they are often not as price-sensitive as larger customers. And if they do leave, there's a low cost to the business since they generate low revenue and margin.

Yellow = Medium Risk.

Red = High Risk. There is a higher risk of them leaving over a price increase since they are often quite price-sensitive. And the cost to the company is high if they do leave because they are the source of a lot of revenue and profit.-

The numbers inside the dots represent the number of customers in each segment. In the example shown in Figure 15.2, we see that 769 customers each bought less than $15,000 in revenue at less than 30 percent gross margin. And only seven customers bought over $75,000 each in revenue at greater than 50 percent gross margin. Of course, there will always be many more customers in the lower-left-hand corner than in the upper right.

How to Use This Tool

There is a ton of opportunity in that bottom left-hand corner. In that area, the risk to your organization is low. Those customers individually represent almost no revenue and almost no margin. They're buying far below market price, which means that when you increase their price, most of them will stick around. Incidentally, you don't have to take them all the way up to where your strategy says they should be; just take them up to average or even just a few points apiece, and this will generate real financial benefit for you. Green means go! Take action.

If the heat map showed data from your company, you might think you'd want to take action with those 769 customers. That's a great plan if you have 75 sales reps who can each take 10 accounts. But if you have seven sales reps, you might need to cut that corner a little bit tighter because you have limited time and attention to give.

That said, you can afford to be imperfect in the lower-left-hand corner. For this lower-risk segment, fast is better than perfect because lower profits linger as long as you take time to perfect your approach. (As General George Patton once said, "A good plan, violently executed now, is better than a perfect plan next week.") You may not necessarily have to go line by line, product by product, service by service in planning a price increase for these customers.

Generally, the further up and to the right, the more risk there is: red means caution! That is not to say that there is no pricing opportunity there, but you want to tread carefully. Those are large, high-margin customers, so making slower and highly calibrated decisions is warranted. Unlike the lower left, fast isn't better. Don't tarry, but do take the time necessary to consider their pricing very carefully and strategically.

Just as with the Scatter Plot, this tool helps you quickly identify where you can move a little faster and with a little less effort while still taking very little risk. Bullets before cannonballs. Take action in low-risk areas, learn, calibrate, and move on to bigger opportunities.

Download the Revenue-Margin Heat Map Tool here:

Tool 3: Pareto Chart

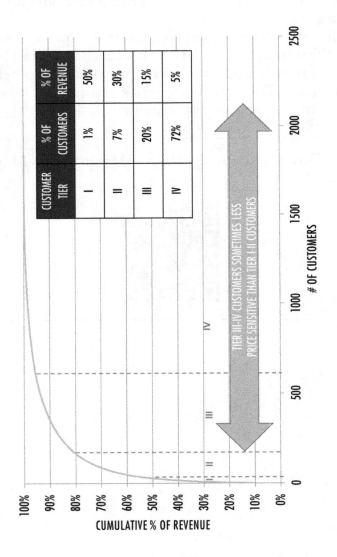

Figure 15.3 Pareto Chart: Customers

Everyone knows the 80/20 rule, also known as the Pareto principle. This Pareto Chart is a simple way to show what percentage of your customers makes up what percentage of your revenue. Like the Revenue-Margin Scatter and Heat Map, the Pareto Chart is a focusing tool that allows you to zero in on opportunity.

I break customer volume into four tiers:

- Tier I: Top 50% of sales volume
- Tier II: Next 30% of sales volume
- Tier III: Next 15% of sales volume
- Tier IV: Last 5% of sales volume

When I share this tool with sales teams, using data from every client who bought from them in the last year—from the customer who bought $7.67 to the customer who bought $767,000—it does not surprise them to see that a relatively small percentage of their customers made up a big chunk of their revenue. That very small number of very large customers is where they're spending a lot of time, effort, energy, and worry. (Appropriately so.)

In Figure 15.3, reflecting real data from one of our clients, 8 percent of customers account for 80 percent of the revenue. If we break that into the tier categories above, 1 percent of the company's customers represents 50 percent of its revenue. The next 30 percent of its revenue comes from 7 percent of its customers. So, for this company, the top 8 percent of its customers make up 80 percent of its revenue. The next 15 percent of revenue comes from 20 percent of its customers.

The big opportunity exists in the last 5 percent of their revenue. That last 5 percent comes from 72 percent of their customers. These are customers who called them and requested a quote. The company had to set up each of these customers in the system. For each customer, they created a quote, requiring design work, cost estimation, and other time-consuming internal steps. They spent sales time and effort. They manufactured each customer's order and then picked, packed, and shipped the order. They issued invoices. They processed payments. All that work for a full 72 percent of their customers made up just 5 percent of their revenue. Painful.

This client knew the work to manage a tiny customer wasn't tiny *enough*. While it's less than the work to manage a large customer, it's not proportionally less. In other words, a customer buying $10,000 per year doesn't take 99 percent less work than a customer buying $1,000,000 per year, even though they generate 99 percent less revenue. Even with small customers paying a higher price, true net profitability, when this cost-to-serve is factored in, is often less than larger customers.

How to Use This Tool

Typically, understanding the market price and what customers are willing to pay largely comes from the tier I and tier II customers. They're the biggest buyers, the squeaky wheels, the vocal minority, so they tend to set our measure of "what the market will bear." But that causes us to underprice to the tier III and IV customers.

Frequently, tier III and tier IV customers are less sensitive than tier I and tier II customers. Those tier III and IV customers are sometimes budget-conscious because they're smaller and counting every penny, but typically, customers in that part of the chart represent a pricing opportunity.

If you're going to do business in that tier IV tail, you must make sure it's worth your while!

Another important thing to note about this chart is that it looks at gross margin, but there are costs to serve a customer not accounted for in gross margin. There is a certain amount of sunk cost in managing and doing business with a customer—like the act of setting a customer up in your system, issuing an invoice, or processing a payment, even if they're only buying $7.67 worth of products from you. The true cost to serve is higher than we measure, and the true benefit to our company for that 72 percent is lower than it looks on paper.

If you could cut out that 72 percent of your customers tomorrow—just stop doing business with them—I believe you would actually be more profitable. You would definitely be more efficient. If you gave up that 5 percent of your revenue, it wouldn't meaningfully affect your company's financials, but it would meaningfully affect how you work and how much time you have to spend. Conserve your sales and operational resources for those customers who are actually paying your bills, which isn't tier IV.

Am I suggesting you should cut off that 5 percent and stop selling to tier IV customers? No, but I am suggesting you should probably get more aggressive in the tail. If you raise prices for those customers or aren't as quick to discount, most of them will stay. And you are going to be better compensated for all those hidden costs-to-serve that you don't account for.

Using the Pareto Chart for Products and Services

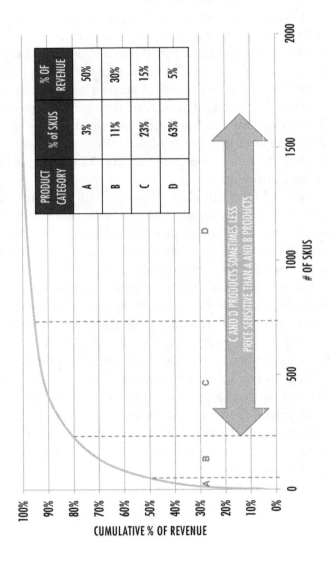

Figure 15.4 Pareto Chart: Products and Services

The Pareto Chart can be used for products and services, too.[†††]

I break product volume into four velocity segments:

A. Top 50% of sales volume
B. Next 30% of sales volume
C. Next 15% of sales volume
D. Last 5% of sales volume

You may have your own breakdown of your products into velocity segments that differs somewhat, but the same principles apply. How much work, time, difficulty, and energy go into the slowest moving products?

A products, and to a lesser degree, B products, are the fastest movers. Those high-velocity movers tend to influence the price sensitivity of their slowest movers. I've heard sales reps talk about a certain margin benchmark as "a good margin." Many companies establish margin targets. The client whose data is shown in Figure 15.4 had a 30 percent margin target. Reps constantly talked to each other, their managers, and even in self-talk about how "30 is a good margin, and 35 is a great margin." This rule of thumb was applied across the business. But guess what? A products, the most sensitive, are the gasoline. (See Chapter 8.) Getting a 30 percent gross margin there probably would be quite good, and getting a 35 percent would be great! But the C and especially the D products are hot sauce. Maybe 40 percent or 50 percent or even higher is possible there without too

---

[†††] *Note:* Velocity metrics are generally applied more for companies selling products than services. As such, for this section, I'll use product and SKU terminology, although the same methodology can be used to identify opportunities in service offerings.

much customer scrutiny. These reps tell themselves that 30 is a good margin because that's what's manageable for the gasoline, but that causes them to underprice the hot sauce.

Also, if 63 percent of your SKUs make up 5 percent of your revenue, as seen in Figure 15.4, why are you still offering all those products? Can you rationalize your product portfolio with this type of analysis? Of course, sometimes you need to keep a very slow-moving SKU to maintain a full product basket. You don't want someone coming to you for 73 of their valves and going to somebody else for the 74th because then it opens the door for competition. I'm not suggesting that you eliminate SKUs you need, but if you're going to keep this low-volume SKU, do it with your eyes wide open. Price it appropriately.

Download the Pareto Chart Tool here:

Tool 4: Pareto Heat Map

REVENUE		CUSTOMER TIERS				
		I	II	III	IV	TOTAL
PRODUCT CATEGORY	A	30% MOST RISK	14%	5%	2%	50%
	B	14%	10%	5%	1%	30%
	C	5%	5%	3%	1%	15%
	D	2%	2%	1%	1% LEAST RISK	5%
	TOTAL	50%	30%	15%	5%	100%

Figure 15.5 Customer-Product Pareto Heat Map

The Pareto Heat Map looks at customers and products together. This map is designed to give a sense of your revenue distribution by customer size and product velocity at the same time. In Figure 15.5, the biggest customers (tier I) buying the fastest-moving products (A) represent 30 percent of revenue.

How to Use This Tool

Even with your A products, typically your very price-sensitive products, arguably your gasoline, you can be a little more aggressive to your tier IV customers. And even with your tier I customers, your biggest and most price-sensitive customers, you can probably be a little more aggressive with your hot sauce products (D products).

Reviewing this data for your company can help you avoid these common underpricing pitfalls:

- Offering low prices to *everyone* buying high-velocity products, even though some smaller customers aren't as sensitive to those products.
- Offering low prices on *every* product sold to high-volume customers, even though some slower-velocity products aren't as sensitive for those customers.

Of course, you must tread carefully with your top-tier customers and your fastest-moving products but don't ignore the opportunity that exists in the other 70 percent of your revenue (or whatever percentage your yellow and green segments make up).

Download the Pareto Heat Map Tool here:

Client Spotlight: Mike Greene, Air Control Products

Is your industry so competitive and commoditized that you can't raise prices?

Mike Greene, the president of Air Control Products, thought so. His father started the company, a manufacturer's rep organization in the HVAC and architectural space, in 1975. In those days, the goal was just to get by. "There wasn't a lot of strategizing being done," he says. "It was all about trying to make a buck, keep the lights on, and keep going."

By the time Greene took over running the business, he says, "my world was pretty sheltered. All I knew was you can only make 'this much' money. That's all anybody's going to pay, and our market is different from everybody else's."

Boost helped teach Air Control Product's team that if you think your stuff is only worth *this much*, that's all it's going to be worth to your customers. But if you provide a superior product or service—as they did—your price should match that.

At the time, the company was not thinking about raising prices. "That was taboo to us," Greene says, "because our position in the market, at that time, was the low-price leader. We thought we had to be low to get the work." As Boost talked about how they could raise prices, the team was apprehensive. But they saw that it was possible and decided to try.

"We started talking about it and adding 1 percent here and adding 2 percent there," Greene says. The seed was planted, and it started to grow. Before long, he says, they were realizing, "Wait a minute—if we're getting more money, that means our service has to be better. Products have to be better. We have to advertise that we're better. We have to show people what they're getting."

Once the sales team understood the total package they offer (leveraging relationships with top-of-line manufacturers, internal expert knowledge, and overall service), their limiting beliefs were destroyed and the company was able to not only raise their prices, but also make their customers feel the value—and believe it's worth the price.

"Recently, a customer did a testimonial. It wasn't even a testimonial for us. He was in a different workshop, and it found its way to me. And he said, 'Mike Greene has done an amazing job with Air Control Products. He's able to train people that aren't in the industry to learn our industry and keep his pricing extremely competitive,'" Greene shares. "It's not that we're extremely competitively priced, but rather the customer feels like they are underpaying for the value we are providing. So, for ten years now [since we first worked with Boost], we just keep doing this."

In an industry where it was believed that "not much was possible" in terms of pricing, Greene and Air Control Products were able to raise their prices and grow their business. "When everybody tells me that's just the way our industry is, well, then we're going to change it," he says. Now, when his salespeople push back on increasing price, Greene challenges them to think, "What if it's possible?"

"It becomes part of your culture," Greene says. "And when your company's culture just talks about this all the time, then you know they've got it."

CHAPTER 16

TOOLS FOR SMART DECISIONS

The previous four tools are designed to focus your team on pricing opportunities in your existing body of business. The tools in this chapter provide pricing guidance to help your team avoid mistakes *as business is priced out* to ensure smart pricing decisions for your business.

In this chapter, we'll look at three tools:

1. Profitability Levers Model
2. Price-Volume Trade-off Table
3. Price-Volume Trade-off Graph

I think of these tools as "what-if" tools. They give a quick picture of business impact from certain decisions related to pricing—increasing price or discounting, for example. They give you a window into the financial future of the decisions you make today.

Tool 5: Profitability Levers Model

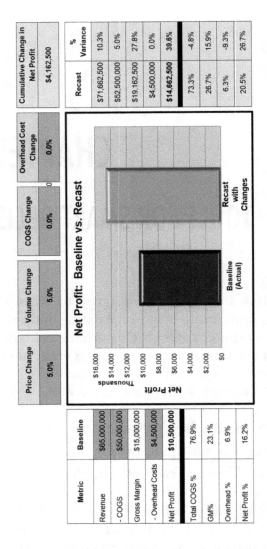

Figure 16.1 Profitability Levers Model

Use this model to recast actual history with changes in price, volume, direct cost, and overhead cost to understand the impact of critical levers for profitability in your company.

This tool helps you understand the impact of critical levers for profitability in your company: price, volume, direct costs, and overhead costs.

To use the tool, populate the yellow cells as follows:

1. Populate Revenue, Cost of Goods Sold (COGS), and Total Overhead Costs on the left-hand side.

2. Input the percent change in Price, Volume, Direct Costs, and Overhead Costs on the top line to see the change in revenue, gross margin, and net profit.

3. Change as many or as few levers at once as you wish. To isolate the impact of just one lever (for example, price), change only that lever and leave the rest at 0 percent change.

How to Use This Tool

Spend some time with the Profitability Levers Model. Play the "what if" game to understand the impact of various decisions and assumptions. If costs go up, what kind of price increase is necessary to stay whole? How much volume can you afford to lose with a price increase and break even? If you can reduce overhead and hold pricing steady, what will happen to your profit?

Share it with your sales team. (Don't share net profit information with your team today? See the note in Chapter 1 on this topic so your team understands the costliness of discounting and the power of small increases regardless of the level of financial visibility at your company.) Do they understand the trade-off between price and volume and the impact on profitability? Commonly, this is vaguely understood in a general way but poorly understood in a specific way, leading to the "we'll make it up in volume" attitude that leads to less profitability.

Ensure that each person who makes selling and pricing decisions clearly understands the cost to the business from a small change in price:

- What does a 5 percent discount cost in gross margin and net margin?
- How much positive impact does a 5 percent price increase have on the gross margin and net margin?
- What volume impact offsets that change? (If you won't lose that amount of sales volume with the price increase, you're still money ahead.)

Make this exercise personal by asking them to calculate the impact on sales commissions. This is a powerful motivator, especially if the salesperson is paid in whole or in part on margin. (Even for revenue-based commissions, higher prices drive higher revenues, so help your team understand how they can make more money by applying these principles.)

Download the Profitability Levers Model here:

Tool 6: Price-Volume Trade-Off Table

PRICE CHANGE	PRESENT GROSS MARGIN										
	10%	15%	20%	25%	30%	35%	40%	45%	50%	55%	60%
	SALES VOLUME CHANGE FOR BREAKEVEN										
20%	-67%	-57%	-50%	-44%	-40%	-36%	-33%	-31%	-29%	-27%	-25%
15%	-60%	-50%	-43%	-37%	-33%	-30%	-27%	-25%	-23%	-21%	0%
10%	-50%	-40%	-33%	-29%	-25%	-22%	-20%	-18%	-17%	-15%	-14%
5%	-33%	-25%	-20%	-17%	-14%	-11%	-11%	-10%	-9%	-8%	-8%
2%	-17%	-12%	-9%	-7%	-6%	-5%	-5%	-4%	-4%	-4%	-3%
1%	-9%	-6%	-5%	-4%	-3%	-3%	-2%	-2%	-2%	-2%	-2%
-1%	11%	7%	5%	4%	3%	3%	3%	2%	2%	2%	2%
-2%	25%	15%	11%	9%	7%	6%	5%	5%	4%	4%	3%
-5%	100%	50%	33%	25%	20%	17%	14%	12%	11%	10%	9%
-10%		200%	100%	67%	50%	40%	33%	29%	25%	22%	20%
-15%			300%	150%	100%	75%	60%	50%	43%	37%	33%
-20%				400%	200%	133%	100%	80%	67%	57%	50%

Figure 16.2 Price-Volume Trade-Off Table

The purpose of this tool is to help you understand what your profit picture will look like if you raise prices and lose volume or discount to stimulate volume growth.

This table serves as a quick reference guide with the same type of data revealed in the profit levers calculator. It illustrates the relationship between price and volume to break even at various gross margins. It's a tool you can use at the moment when a salesperson says, "I think we can grow volume by 10 percent if we do this for 5 percent less!" With gross margins of 25 percent, for example, you can quickly see that this is a bad decision. A 5 percent discount on a 25 percent gross margin product means you must increase sales volume by 25 percent just to maintain identical profitability. In other words, you make more money with current pricing and volume than you would by discounting 5 percent for 10 percent volume growth.

I used to have this break-even table on my desk when I was a pricing manager for Glidden because I found it to be a helpful tool to share with people during pricing discussions. Once, Jim, the product manager for our related products—paintbrushes, rollers, plastic sheeting, and so on—came to me and said, "I want to run a promotion in March for related products. I really want to get a bunch of sales rolling, and I want to do a 10 percent discount." I knew our gross margin for sheeting was about 20 percent. So, I pulled out this table, and I saw that a 10 percent discount at 20 percent gross margin meant we would have to double our sales to make the same amount. I asked Jim, "How much sales volume do you think you could bump with a promotion like this?" He said, "I think 30 percent!" And I said, "Unless there's another nonquantifiable, nonfinancial strategic reason to do this, I would recommend against it." What I thought was: *No stinking way are we going to run this promotion! It will lose us money!*

Looking at the table, you can see how the top part builds confidence: a 20 percent price increase on a 25 percent gross margin product means you can lose almost half of your sales and still make as much money. It helps you put boundaries around the risk so that you can be confident enough to take action.

> **There can be business reasons to do things that are bad for your numbers. But you'd better do them with your eyes open.**

In the lower half of the table, you are getting into dangerous territory. And the grayed-out part of the table is where it is impossible to break even and maintain profitability, no matter the combination. There is no volume increase big enough to allow you to break even on a 10 percent discount at 10 percent gross margin. For every unit you sell there, you lose *more* money.

Download the Price-Volume Trade-Off Graph here:

Tool 7: Price-Volume Trade-Off Graph

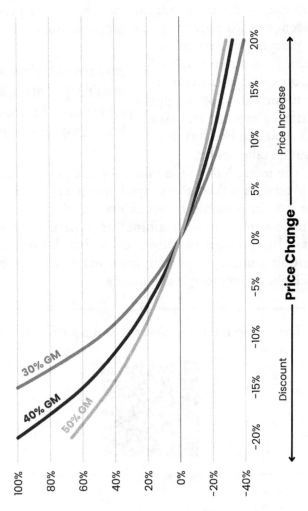

Figure 16.3 Price-Volume Trade-Off Graph

This tool uses the same information as the Price-Volume Trade-Off Table but presents it graphically. Looking at the graph, you can see that a 10 percent price increase at 30 percent gross margin means you can lose 25 percent of your sales volume and still break even. For that same product, a 10 percent discount means you need to sell 50 percent more product to break even.

The Price-Volume Trade-Off Graph provides a graphical view of the data in the table, helping you make a smart decision for your business.

Download the Price-Volume Trade-Off Table here:

Client Spotlight: Keith Elphick, Airline Hydraulics

How do you make pricing a focal point of your business? For Keith Elphick, director of sales at Airline Hydraulics, a distributor and manufacturer of automation and hydraulic products systems, it takes three things: a pricing czar, constant education, and frequent reminders to salespeople of the value they bring.

Airline's salesforce is split between a fluid hydraulics team and an automation team. More than 40 salespeople are responsible for 70-100 accounts each. The struggle for salespeople is always wanting to drop the price to make the sale. "They think they've got an intuition or gut feeling; they think they've got to lower their price. It's an everyday thing in sales. The people we hire are smart, very technical engineering salespeople. But they still don't connect [price] with the value we bring."

That's where the three pricing tactics come in.

The pricing czar "really helps with salespeople's understanding," Elphick says. "You've got to spend the money and have this person who is in charge of all the price files and where we go with the margins." The company puts a certain margin on all its value-add projects, and if a sales rep wants to lower that margin, they have to give the pricing czar a reason.

"I really want the salespeople to articulate the value they bring, and what does life look like to that customer if they don't have you?" Elphick explains. "We've worked on medical projects that save thousands, and sales reps want to lower the price. I say, 'Well, what's the reason?' [And they say,] 'It's just a gut feeling.' A gut feeling doesn't work in our business—you've got to have some good facts."

Once the salesperson articulates a relevant reason to lower the price, they'll get a passcode to lower the margin. They are then locked into that price.

When it comes to education, Elphick says they continuously try to hammer home with salespeople the ideas of identifying where customers aren't paying attention and doing fractional increases and discounts.

"Just yesterday, we had a customer tell us that a price was too high. And the first thing I told the sales rep was, 'Well, ask him what features they don't want.'" And at the end of the conversation, [the customer] *added* features, and the price even went up higher than it was," Elphick says. "There's not a month that goes by that we don't talk about hot sauce when we're raising prices. Let's raise the prices on the things that people don't realize. They care about the price of extrusion per inch. But they don't care about the bolt that puts it together."

Price is something that buyers feel they can negotiate on, he says. "It sounds like they're asking for it cheaper sometimes, but they don't know what they're asking. They don't know what they're even getting that they're asking for cheaper. And as we've learned, buyers are liars." He reminds his salespeople that instead of lowering price to meet a customer's request, they can do a fractional discount. "Maybe 15 days net terms and set the price to give them a little win, or maybe something in between. But we try not to because if we're lowering our price that quickly, then [they think] we were gouging them from the start."

In the same way, they can raise prices fractionally. "On a $70 item, a half a percent is 35 cents. Nobody's going to knock you down for 35 cents," he says.

Having a pricing czar to keep people on track and providing constant education on pricing is valuable, but reminding salespeople about the value they bring is just as critical. "You've got to teach them to value what they're doing for the customer, all the time they're spending, and why they're special," he says. Because if they don't know that and don't operate out of that belief, they easily fall into the trap of unnecessarily discounting.

As the sales leader, Elphick is always reminding his team that they are the best at what they do and that their customers know that. "Salespeople want to give everything away for free," he says. "There's not a day that goes by, including four times yesterday, that I don't tell our people, 'But you are Picasso! Don't give it away.'" The other way he reminds them of their value is to ask if they got a love letter—a sign that the customer is "dying to buy from you."

"We get love letters every day because customers love our people. But if you're not getting that, you haven't gotten to their core yet, where they see you as that value."

The best way to focus on value with the customer, Elphick says, is to focus on the benefit of what you sell. When a CFO picks up a quote, they may not know what the product is that you're quoting, but they will understand how it benefits their business. "Don't tell me what you're selling; tell me how it benefited somebody because that's going to benefit somebody else. Don't tell the [CFO] that you're selling a hydraulic power unit. Tell him their production is going to go up by two times because they're going to use this new efficient system."

Making pricing a focal point of their business has paid off for Airline in increased margins and profitability. But it's an ongoing process. Elphick says, "It's gentle pressure applied relentlessly. And some [salespeople] are really learning; some of them still fall off the bicycle every day. And we've just got to teach them how to ride again."

CONCLUSION

I deliver keynotes all over the world, and I ask a set of questions at the beginning of the talk and again at the end. One question I ask before and after is "How much pricing power do you have?" (Specifically, how much pricing power do you have in *your* market with *your* customers relative to *your* competition?)

The answers, at the beginning, generally skew toward "very little power." At the end, the answer is much different, skewed more toward "a lot of power." For example, here are the aggregated results from three years of my keynotes to over 7,500 CEO audience members collectively:

HOW MUCH PRICING POWER DO YOU HAVE?

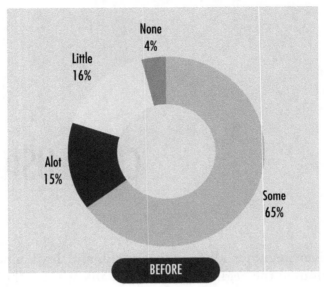

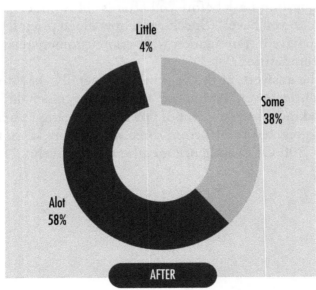

Each time this "transformation" of their pricing power is revealed, I joke with audiences that a miracle occurred while we were in the keynote: Their industry shifted. Their market changed. And their customers became far less price-sensitive.

Of course, they know that nothing changed in the marketplace. Instead, everything changed in the minds of the people in that room.

It is an exciting moment for me, every single time, because real dollars are at stake. Henry Ford said, "If you think you can or you think you can't, you're right." It's our beliefs about our pricing power that stop us short. Our beliefs can propel us to ask for higher prices. Or they can cause us to fall back and discount, conceding prices from fear.

These before-and-after results are the proof of what I have said throughout this book: the primary reason companies are not making more money with pricing isn't the customer. It isn't the competition. It's us. It's our own fear and lack of confidence. Our customers would have us believe that our prices are too high because they want

> Our beliefs can propel us to ask for higher prices. Or they can cause us to fall back and discount, conceding prices from fear.

to hold on to their dollars. But their money-saving agenda isn't a true measure of your value or your pricing power.

If I were to ask you the same question before and after reading this book, I think your answers would trend in the same way. Like those audience members, you now know that *you*, in large part, determine your pricing power, through your preparation and your confidence in your value story. You are undervaluing and underpricing your products and services every day, reinforced by customers telling you that your prices are too high.

I'm not saying that you can raise prices simply because you want to or think you can. You still need a careful plan to increase prices in a strategic, risk-mitigated way. You may be underestimating your ability to increase pricing on some products or services, on some things you give away, and to some customers. It's costing your profitability dearly.

I hope this book has shown you that, as a company that produces quality, service, and excellence, you already have the power to charge more. You don't need a perfect pricing strategy. You already have pricing power. Have the confidence to act on that power.

Increase Your Profitability in One Hour

If you do only one thing after reading this book, I ask you to give just a little more time and attention to price execution.

With all the chaos that businesses have gone through during the past several years—from the pandemic to shutdowns to record levels of demand to supply chain interruptions to the war for talent to soaring inflation— many have found it takes a lot more time and effort to sell and serve their customers. You're on a hamster wheel of selling and then serving, selling and then serving, and you're doing it well. You never want to fall off the wheel because you can't afford not to sell, and you certainly will never be the kind of company that doesn't deliver with excellence.

The problem arises when you're so busy selling and serving and delivering and executing that price management gets the least focus. Ensure you're being surgical and strategic about every pricing decision you make; maximize every 0.5 percent, 1 percent, 2 percent, on every product or service on every proposal for every customer. Don't simply slap on the same old margins or prices you did before.

Take a pause from the hamster wheel and ask, "Am I being paid well to work this hard?" Don't be a worn out, bedraggled hamster.

Indulge me in a thought exercise.

1. Think about how many hours you spent last week on sales-related activities. Everything from meeting with customers to internal sales-related meetings to preparing bids and proposals—everything you did to grow and manage sales. How many hours did you spend, or what percentage of your week did you spend? When you have that number, write it down.

2. Now, think about how many hours you spent chasing labor, product, and everything it takes to make sure your customers are well served—the execution side, the delivery side of your promise. How many hours did you spend or what percentage of your week? Write that down. (For many of you right now who are running faster than ever, it probably feels like you've already hit 200 percent.)

3. Finally, how many hours a week are you spending on surgical and strategic profitable pricing decision-making and planning? Now, I don't mean, "Hey, we have a brand-new customer opportunity. What price will it take to win it?" Or "How should we price this SKU or project?" Those are tactical discussions and decisions, and they're important. I know you think and talk about pricing and margins all the time. But at a strategic level, how much time and effort are you spending on pricing?

That means understanding trends and metrics and what they mean, inside and outside the business. It means noticing that win rates are starting to drop for your OEM customers on stainless steel products and exploring that early warning signal about price sensitivity, competition, and so on. Or finding that deals are taking longer to close than they did six months ago and jumping on that to understand what is happening in the market. What do these situations mean for your pricing?

How much time goes into strategic price management and price execution? For many organizations, it's virtually zero, or literally zero, but even if it's 10 percent of your time, it's always the smallest chunk of your focus.

This is the most profitable way to spend an hour this week. Put one more hour of your week into thinking about and looking at strategic pricing for your business and exploring pricing metrics and trends. Spend time talking to your salespeople about it, looking at the pricing decisions they're making, and having more conversations about it.

It's so easy for pricing to get lost in the shuffle during the busyness of business. Giving it just one more hour of your time and attention is a simple way to start acting on your pricing power. Put it on your calendar. Just one more hour.

Be a well-paid hamster.

ACKNOWLEDGMENTS

This book wouldn't be in your hands today without the love, support, and inspiration of so many incredible people.

To my partner Jeff, and our beautiful kids Kyle, Alex, Kira, and Lia—you are my reason for everything I do. Jeff, thank you for being my rock, my greatest champion, and my constant source of balance. And to our kids, you remind me every day what's most important.

To Mom, Dad, and my brothers—you have shaped me, taught me, loved me, and believed in me. I love you all so much.

To my dear friends in the entrepreneurial community, my mentors, and my coaches—Alex Freytag, Christy Clement, Bridget Murphy, Lorene Haimerl, Juan Alvarez, Ruth Milligan, Beth Menduni, and Greg Black. You have guided me, challenged me, and helped me grow in ways I never imagined. You pushed me to think bigger, dig deeper, and never settle for less than excellence. I am honored to be part of such a vibrant, powerful network. Thank you.

To the organizations and communities that have shaped my thinking and development—Vistage Worldwide with Working Surface, Strategic Coach® with Dan Sullivan, and EOS® Worldwide with Gino Wickman. Your frameworks, tools, and teachings have been transformative. Gino, thank you for your generous and thoughtful foreword to this book.

To the clients who generously shared their stories for this book—Vern Hydorn, Steve Voelzke, Reid Hutchison, Peter Argondizzo, Mike Greene, Matt Crenshaw, Marnie Ochs-Raleigh, Keith Elphick, Joe Parker, Brent Darnell, Brad Tinney, Bob Domnick, Betsy McLarney, Beka Eisenbarth, Andy Schuster, and Alec Broadfoot—you have not only been clients, but also friends, mentors, and inspirations. Your trust and openness in sharing your experiences have enriched this book immeasurably.

To my network who jumped in immediately when I asked for book endorsements—thank you for your early support and lending your powerful bylines to the book to help me reach a wider audience.

To my team at Boost Pricing, both past and present—your dedication, passion, and commitment are nothing short of inspiring. You are the heartbeat of our mission to help businesses be paid well for their excellence. I'm endlessly grateful to be on this journey with you.

To Heidi Hill, my extraordinary developmental editor—thank you for turning my raw ideas into a cohesive, powerful narrative. Thanks for pushing me through the toughest parts of writing this book! I'm lucky to call you a friend.

To Kary, Sarah, Lori, Teri, Jill, and the rest of the Igniting Souls organization—thank you for believing in this book and for guiding me through the publishing process with such grace and enthusiasm.

To all the rest of my family and friends, whose names aren't mentioned here but whose presence is always felt—thank you from the bottom of my heart. You've rallied behind me time and again. I am honored and grateful to have each of you in my life.

And finally, to every reader who picks up this book—thank you for joining me on this journey. I hope it inspires you to recognize your own worth, to charge confidently for your excellence, and to never settle for less than you deserve.

With heartfelt gratitude,
Casey

NOTES

Chapter 1

Jeanne Hedden Gallagher. "Consumers Prefer Round Numbers Even When the Specific Number Is Better News." *Rensselaer Polytechnic Institute.* July 6, 2020. https://news.rpi.edu/content/2020/07/06/consumers-prefer-round-numbers-even-whe n-specific-number-better-news.

Chapter 3

David R. Henderson. "Demand." *The Library of Economics and Liberty.* https://stageeconlib.wpengine.com/library/Enc/Demand.html. Accessed September 17, 2024.

Chapter 4

John Harrison. "19 Inspirational Quotes about Pricing." *Aimondo.com.* August 2, 2023. https://www.aimondo.com/en/article/19-inspirational-quotes-about-pricing.

Chapter 6

Associated Press. "'Pharma Bro' Martin Shkreli is ordered to return $64M, barred from drug industry." *NPR.org.* January 14, 2022. https://www.npr.org/2022/01/14/1073161736/pharma-bro-martin-shkreli-barred.

Christopher E. Ondeck and John R. Ingrassia. "$264 Million Settlement in EpiPen Price Gouging Litigation." *The National Law Review.* July 22, 2022. https://natlawreview.com/article/264-million-settlement-epipen-price-gouging-litigation.

"Price Gouging Complaints Surge Amid Coronavirus Pandemic." *New York Times.* March 27, 2020. https://www.nytimes.com/2020/03/27/us/coronavirus-price-gouging-hand-sanitizer-masks-wipes.html

Chapter 9

Tracie Chancellor. "Selling the Sizzle, Not the Steak, Still Works." May 14, 2020. https://telereach.com/selling-the-sizzle-not-the-steak-still-works/#:~:text=In%20the%201950's%20a%20salesman,work%20from%20home%20in%20sales.

Charles Revson. "In the factory, we manufacture cosmetics; in the store we sell hope." *Quoteswise.com.* http://www.quoteswise.com/charles-revson-quotes.html.

Paul Hague. "Do Emotions Play a Part in Business-to-Business in Decision Making?" *B2B International.com.* https://www.b2binternational.com/publications/emotions-in-business-to-business-decision-making/. Accessed September 17, 2024.

Fortune Knowledge Group and Gyro. "Only Human: The Emotional Logic of Business Decision." executive summary. 2014. https://datascienceassn.org/sites/default/files/Only%20Human%20-%20The%20Emotional%20Logic%20of%20Business%20Decisions.pdf.

Sam Nathan and Karl Schmidt. "From Promotion to Emotion: Connecting B2B Customers to Brands." ThinkWithGoogle.com. October 2014. https://www.laughlin.com/Laughlin/media/public/img/ideas/CEB_Promotion_to_Emotion_whitepaper.pdf.

Michael E. Gerber. *The E-Myth Revisited: Why Most Small Businesses Don't Work and What to Do About It.* New York: HarperCollins, 2009.

Chapter 10

GoodCarBadCar. "U.S. Automotive Sales Data" in "Global Automotive Sales Data." https://www.goodcarbadcar.net/. Accessed September 17, 2024. Various automotive data sites report slight differences in unit growth over this timeframe, but all compared sources report well over 30 percent growth in Hyundai sales in the U.S. This book relied on U.S. unit data for 2008, 2009, and 2010.

Chapter 12

Bruce Lee. "The Lost Interview." Interview by
Pierre Berton. *The Pierre Berton Show*. December 9,
1971. Available on YouTube.com. https://youtu.be/
uk1lzkH-e4U?feature=shared.

Chapter 15

Jim Collins and Morten T. Hansen. *Great by Choice:
Uncertainty, Chaos, and Luck—Why Some Thrive Despite
Them All*. New York: HarperCollins, 2011.

ABOUT THE AUTHOR

Casey Brown is a pricing geek and professional speaker with a passion to help leaders, entrepreneurs, and sellers to command the prices they deserve. As the founder of Boost Pricing, she leads a team of experts who help companies sell at higher prices to drive profitable growth. Through her consulting work and keynotes, Casey demystifies customer tactics and arms sellers with practical, ready-to-implement steps to negotiate fearlessly, price confidently, and own their value.

Casey's decades-long reputation as a pricing expert arose from pioneering innovative content, formulating and executing pricing strategies, and coaching and training teams to drive sustainable results. She has helped over 1,000 companies generate more than \$1 billion in incremental profits.

Casey holds degrees in Chemical Engineering, Spanish, and Business, is fluent in Spanish, and is a certified Six Sigma Black Belt. Outside of her professional pursuits, she founded a nonprofit organization that funds life-changing cleft lip and palate surgeries in Guatemala and dedicates over 600 hours annually to volunteer work focused on meeting children's basic needs.

Her TEDx talk has been viewed nearly 4 million times. Casey lives in Columbus, Ohio, with her family.

CONNECT WITH CASEY

Follow her on LinkedIn for pricing tips, free resources, and more.

LINKEDIN.COM/IN/CASEYBROWNBOOST